"*Hunting Magic Eels* is a wonder insightful book. Tapping into both his training as a psychologist and the treasures within an array of Christian traditions, Richard Beck prescribes a way to begin healing from the ache and skepticism we feel in our disenchanted age. By attending to the wonder, beauty, and mystery of everyday life, Beck calls us to rediscover the enchanted world we find ourselves in and the living God who is calling us home."

—**Joshua Chatraw**, The Billy Graham Chair of Evangelism and Cultural Engagement, Beeson Divinity School

"*Hunting Magic Eels* is a much-needed message of hope for sharing faith in a skeptical and secular age. Beck reminds us of the rich resources in the Christian traditions to reinvigorate not only our churches but our personal journeys of faith. After reading *Hunting Magic Eels* and his personal stories with the prison Bible study, I am changed forever. It came at just the right time in my faith, giving me language to move from critic of the church and join Beck as a preacher of hope."

—**Lars Coburn**, director of University Relations, Bushnell University

"As a pastor, I found *Hunting Magic Eels* to be an important and creative resource for our faith community as we spent time engaging the 'enchantments' Richard Beck describes. In a skeptical, critical, and divided age, the book gave language that united the longings of our faith community and engaged those longings in real and tangible ways."

—**Molly Conaway**, lead pastor, Crossings faith community,
Knoxville, Tennessee

"Like so many others, I've been reading and learning from Richard Beck for going on two decades. How many can claim to have mastered a discipline outside one's formal training? This psychologist is the best theologian on our shared campus. Whether he's in the classroom, in Sunday school, in a prison, or on the page, Beck is the same: curious, open-minded, open-hearted, wise, insightful, and weird. His truth-seeking and truth-telling are always aslant. This book is no different. In it we discover, or rediscover, a creation charged with the glory of Jesus Christ. Conservatives read Beck because he calls them away from dead letters into the life of the Spirit; liberals read him because he calls them away from disenchantment into the living word and world of God. Whatever you call yourself, you should read him too. You will not be disappointed. You will be surprised."

—**Brad East**, associate professor of theology,
Abilene Christian University, and the author of
The Church's Book and *The Doctrine of Scripture*

"Drawing on his deep insight into the human condition, and years of teaching and pastoring, Richard Beck, in *Hunting Magic Eels*, offers an essential guide to a life of faith in a world dominated by skepticism and scientism. Beck equips the reader to understand the pattern of our disenchanted age, to grasp the faith commitments of secularity, and to reinvigorate Christian faith in a way that is both confident and gracious. The book is a call to pay attention to the God who created our enchanted world and so to live in awareness of the magical life that surrounds us."

—Dr. Joel D. Lawrence, executive director,
Center for Pastor Theologians

"We've grown deeply dissatisfied with disenchantment, whether we know it or not. We lack the ability to face failure, pain, and setback, but don't realize how this is connected to our loss of God. In *Hunting Magic Eels* Richard Beck points us to a faith that provides meaning in these adversities, helping us overcome our blindness to what's right in front of us. Here is a book about a faith that can re-enchant you to the God who is all around you."

—Luke Norsworthy, pastor, author, and
host of the *Newsworthy with Norsworthy* podcast

"Rarely do I find myself moved by the mind of another. Call it intellectual exhaustion. When you read a lot, you secretly long for those works that can wake you up from your slumber. Look no further: *Hunting Magic Eels* is a tonic for the soul and a salve for the heart. Richard Beck masterfully invites us to, once again, gaze at our world in wonder and look skeptically at the hollow ideologies that rob transcendence from our minds. I can't recommend Beck and his mind enough. Nor can I recommend this book more joyfully. This book makes me see the world as a Christian again.

—**A.J. Swoboda**, associate professor of Bible, theology, and world Christianity, Bushnell University, and author of *After Doubt*

"When I sit with folks in spiritual direction and invite their souls into speech, they slowly begin to whisper of mysterious, intimate encounters with the Divine— experiences that don't square with the hyperrational faith nor the evidence-based scientific model we've been given. And yet, Spirit keeps showing up in wildly surprising, mystical ways. Richard Beck articulates a thoughtful, compelling path for moving through life with eyes and heart open to whatever truth and beauty may emerge, allowing ourselves to once again be enchanted by the Divine."

—**Mallory Wyckoff**, writer, spiritual director, and peacemaker

Hunting Magic Eels

Recovering an

Enchanted Faith in

a Skeptical Age

HUNTING

MAGIC

EELS

RICHARD BECK

BROADLEAF BOOKS
MINNEAPOLIS

HUNTING MAGIC EELS
Recovering an Enchanted Faith in a Skeptical Age

First paperback edition published in 2024
by Broadleaf Books.

All Scripture quotations, unless otherwise indicated, are taken from the New Revised Standard Version Bible © 1989 Division of Christian Education of the National Council of the Churches of Christ in the United States of America. Used by permission.

Excerpt from "For Domestic Days" on page 152 is from *Every Moment Holy, Volume 1* by Douglas Kaine McKelvey (Rabbit Room Press 2017), www.EveryMomentHoly.com.

Library of Congress Control Number: 2022276483 (print)

Cover image: eel: Navalnyi/shutterstock / fillagree: standa_art/shutterstock
Cover design: Olga Grlic; 1517 Media

Print ISBN: 978-1-5064-8767-0
eBook ISBN: 979-8-8898-3164-8

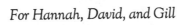

For Hannah, David, and Gill

CONTENTS

PART 3
ENCHANTED CHRISTIANITIES

PART 4
DISCERNING THE SPIRITS

FOREWORD
HUNTING MAGIC EELS

Like hail gently tapping on the roof of a mobile home, my prayer beads tap rhythmically against the edges of my laptop keyboard. Prayer beads are new for me. I thought a long time about wearing prayer beads—or regularly using any tool that might invite me into the contemplative life—as a reminder of the nearness of God, but I never pulled the trigger. It seemed to me, well, strange.

I was raised in a church tradition where those kinds of mnemonic devices weren't considered meaningful. In fact, they were suspect, and perhaps signs of divergent and unbiblical faith. My early religious training taught that a faithful life should be filled with Bible reading, biblical and cultural exegesis, and other practices that filled my mind with much to consider, but few contemplative practices to *do*. There was even less in my spiritual upbringing to *feel*. It was a "rational" religion. Rational meant deploying a particular kind of thinking—a kind that, when done "correctly," simply amplified the concretized conclusions of the men who came before me (and, yes, they were all men). What there was to do outside of thinking was centered on justice and occasional acts of service, but not *too much* justice and not *too much* service. These guardrails kept us from veering toward "the social gospel." And as it turns out, those same guardrails kept many from discovering the height, depth, and breadth of God.

We were mind people. And mind people *only*. To "love the Lord your God with all of our heart, soul, mind, and strength" (see Mark 12:30) meant to love the Lord your God with your mind. Full stop. But even then, only *part* of your mind. There was no space for the contemplative life. There was no such thing as the contemplative life. Likewise, there was little space for mysticism or *experiencing* God. Following Jesus was adherence to denominational practices and preordained questions and answers. It was silly, I believed, that God or Jesus or spirituality might exist in ways not chronicled in rhythms that could be dissected in a Bible class. I was told, quite plainly, that God *only* worked through the pages of Scripture. That explanation worked for me until I graduated college and began vocational ministry.

Outside the confines of the college, I was dropped among people who had different experiences than mine. They invited me into new experiences of how they understood and knew God. I was broadened through thoughtful, beautiful, and God-revealing liturgy. I encountered people who healed and had been healed, not at a televangelist's crusade, but through the prayers of faithful women and men and through the laying on of hands. These experiences opened me to the possibility that God was up to more in the world than my spiritual training could account for, but I had never been trained to see it. And while the experiences of other Christians opened me to a broader range of experiences of God, it was my experience with former Christians that broke me, broke me open, and explains my prayer beads. Other believers had something I didn't. They had a faith I lacked.

In my earliest days of vocational ministry, there was a young girl in my student ministry, Angelica. When she was in tenth grade, Angelica began dating a boy and brought him with her to worship one Sunday. I was leading worship and thought I'd put together a fairly meaningful and impacting gathering. Angelica's boyfriend should have been impressed.

He wasn't.

I asked Angelica the following Wednesday night what her new boyfriend thought about worship. She looked at me, wanting to be honest but also hoping to spare my feelings. She said, "Well, he told me, 'The most you do at your church is stand up and sit down.'"

Bam! That stung.

It stung because Angelica was one of my favorite students and I'd embarrassed her in front of her new boyfriend. It was doubly biting because I knew it was true. I had done what I knew to do. I also knew it was limited and that God was broader and deeper, but I didn't know how to experience for myself nor invite others into it. And I am not alone.

Church life, not just for Angelica's boyfriend but for me and many others over the past twenty or so years, has felt limiting and left us wanting. We've stood up and sat down, stood up and sat down for decades and can no longer avoid noticing all the space a curtailed and narrow expectation and experience of God create. We noticed what, for so long, we have failed to notice.

It is no wonder, then, that church attendance is falling and churches and their leaders are failing.[1] There's plenty of blame to go around. It's easy to blame the public failures of well-known megachurch pastors who have faltered at the basic behaviors of simple Christian practice. Add to that American evangelicals' unholy marriage with political partisanship, and our current circumstance is not surprising. But there may well be a more accessible reason, a reason that contributes to the ennui of the faithful and the lack of believability from those outside church doors. As children of the Enlightenment and products of a consumeristic, mass production–driven culture, Christian practice has been reduced to "standing up and sitting down."

---

1 Jeffrey M. Jones, "U.S. Church Membership Falls Below Majority for First Time," *Gallup*, March 29, 2021, https://news.gallup.com/poll/341963/church-membership-falls-below-majority-first-time.aspx.

Christianity has lost its enchantment.

Richard Beck helps us rediscover our lost enchantment. In this book, Richard offers us the opportunity to immerse ourselves in the enchanted Christian faith that has always been with us, lying in wait. In these pages you will find a faith that not merely acknowledges enchantment, but re-centers the enchanted, mystical world God created—a world of wonder and awe as a mechanism for meaning-making, as well as an apologetic for the witness of the church and work of God.

For ten weeks I, and several other voices in my church, walked our community through the powerful and beautiful truths you will discover in these pages. In the process, our community discovered both relief and freedom. Many were relieved by the truth that their experiences of God—experiences they were slow to speak about publicly—were accurate and true, testifying to the reality of God's work in their lives. Others discovered freedom in embracing the work of God in their lives in ways that might not fit neatly into their inherited categories. In both relief and freedom, they discovered a beautiful, powerful, mysterious God. They discovered a bigger and more active God, a God calling them to more than standing up and sitting down. They rediscovered God at work in ancient practices, in broadening the horizons of liturgical expression and possibilities, and in the eyes of their children, friends, and neighbors. Some, like me, took on new practices, like wearing prayer beads. In ways big and small we began to pay attention to what was always there, but now we could see it.

—Sean Palmer, author, *Speaking by the Numbers* and teaching pastor, Ecclesia Houston

PREFACE TO THE PAPERBACK EDITION

Thank you to Broadleaf Books for bringing *Hunting Magic Eels* out in a paperback edition and for letting me add four additional chapters. The new chapters for the paperback edition are "Why Good People Need God," "Live Your Beautiful Life," "The Primacy of the Invisible," and "Hexing the Taliban." These new chapters respond to questions I've received since the publication of the book and deepen and expand various points.

A very special thank-you to my dear friend Sean Palmer for his graciousness in writing the foreword for the paperback edition.

Thank you to Elysia Willis and Paul Milbank at Unfold Media (www.unfold.media) for allowing me to share an edited version of the essay "Live Your Beautiful Life," which first appeared as a mutinous musing on the pages of the *YoHo Journal* (www.unfold.media/yo-ho-journals).

Special thanks to my sons, Brenden and Aidan Beck: To Brenden, for introducing me to hard and soft magic in fantasy fiction. To Aidan, for alerting me to Witch-Tok and keeping me abreast of the "Hex the Taliban" movement.

Thank you to Ron Wright for bringing to my attention the connection between enchantment and Martin Buber, and to Mark Sampson for introducing me to the work of Hartmut Rosa.

Bits and pieces of the new chapters appeared first on my blog *Experimental Theology* (https://richardbeck .substack.com/).

Finally, I'm finalizing the last edits for the paperback edition while in Taizé, France, on retreat with my dear friends Hannah and Jojo. As I've sat in the songs and silences of the week, sharing worship with the brothers of Taizé, my reflections keep turning to light. One passage especially, from the Gospel of John, has captured my heart. In John 1:7 the ministry of John the Baptist is described this way: "He came as a witness, to testify to the light."

That is all I hope to do in these pages.

To bear witness to the light.

July 2022

Taizé, France

INTRODUCTION
STRANGE SIGHTS

We were hunting for magic eels.

That's an odd opening for a conversation about revitalizing Christian faith in our secular, skeptical age. But stay with me.

The magic eels—or to be more precise, the legend concerning them—are from Wales, where we were on holiday with our dear friend Hannah. We were visiting Llanddwyn Island, exploring the ruins of the abbey associated with St. Dwynwen. St. Dwynwen was a fifth-century Celtic saint and is the patron saint of lovers in Wales. Celebrated on January 25, St. Dwynwen's Day is the Welsh version of St. Valentine's Day.

Llanddwyn Island was a famous site of pilgrimage because of its holy well. Inhabiting the well were enchanted eels that could predict your romantic future. According to the legend, if the eels disturbed a token thrown into the well, your lover would be faithful for life. Not surprisingly, the church became very wealthy due to

RICHARD BECK

all the pilgrimages. Who needs premarital counseling when you've got magic eels?

Pilgrimages to Llanddwyn Island began to decline after the Protestant Reformation. Today, St. Dwynwen's church is a ruin. And sadly, there is no longer a well with magic eels. Things have changed a lot over the last five hundred years.

I want to talk about these changes and their impact on faith in a world increasingly dominated by skepticism, doubt, and disbelief. We don't make pilgrimages to holy wells anymore to pray for our marriages. A world stuffed with supernatural wonders seems to be a thing of the past. Our world is secular, skeptical, and scientific.

Five hundred years ago, life was enchanted. God existed, and the devil was real. The world teemed with angels and demons. There were magical creatures and dark, occult forces. It was a world of holy wells and magic eels.

But with the Protestant Reformation and the beginning of the Enlightenment, the world—in the West, at least—has grown increasingly *disenchanted*. We live in a world dominated by science and technology. Increasing numbers of us don't believe in God anymore, to say nothing about believing in the devil or angels. We don't expect miracles. We know that stage magicians aren't sorcerers, that there's a rational explanation behind their "tricks" and "illusions." The world of St. Dwynwen is viewed as quirky and quaint but also naive and superstitious. We've grown up and left those fairy tales behind. Rates of agnosticism and atheism in the United States have been steadily, if slowly, increasing, especially among the young and college educated. There's also the rise of the "nones," people who no longer formally identify with any religious tradition. Our public sphere is increasingly described as secular and "post-Christian."

This rising tide of disenchantment has profoundly affected our religious imaginations. We've lost our capacity for enchantment, our ability to see and experience God as a living, vital presence in our lives. As Thomas Merton once observed in a talk he gave on August 20, 1965,

> Life is this simple. We are living in a world that is absolutely transparent, and God is shining through it all the time. This is not just a fable or a nice story. It is true. If we abandon ourselves to God and forget ourselves, we see it sometimes, and we see it maybe frequently. God manifests Himself everywhere, in everything—in people and in things and in nature and in events. It becomes very obvious that He is everywhere and in everything and we cannot be without Him. You cannot be without God. It's impossible. It's simply impossible. The only thing is that we don't see it.

God is everywhere, *but we don't see it*. This pervasive disenchantment, which affects Christians as much as nonbelievers, poses the single greatest threat to faith and the church in our post-Christian world. How we lost our ability to see God, why we need to recover it, and how we can do that is what I want to share with you.

In his book *The Pastor in a Secular Age: Ministry to People Who No Longer Need a God*, Andrew Root describes our eroding capacity for enchantment as a form of "attention blindness." Root uses the famous "gorilla experiment" from the psychologist Daniel Simons to make the point. You've likely seen the YouTube clip of the gorilla experiment. At the start of the video, you're asked to pay attention to two teams of people passing a basketball back and forth, with the instructions to count how many passes occur. You dutifully do so. And then, at the end of the video, you're asked if you noticed the dancing gorilla. You're a bit shocked by that question. You've seen no gorilla, only people passing a ball back and forth. But the video rewinds and replays, and lo and behold, there in the middle of the passing teams is a dancing gorilla, as plain as day. How could you have missed such an obvious thing?

We miss the obvious, according to Daniel Simons, because when our attention becomes focused on one part of reality, like counting the passes between the teams, we miss other, even very obvious, aspects of life. Like a dancing gorilla. Our attention helps us *see*, but it also *blinds* us.

According to Root, this is what has been happening in our skeptical age. For five hundred years, technology and science have been grabbing and focusing our attention. For very good reasons. We have been awed and blessed by the achievements of science and technology. But this attention to science and technology has hidden other obvious facts about our lives and world. We've been counting the passes between Team Science and Team Technology and lost sight of God, the dancing gorilla right in front of us. Modern disenchantment is due to this attention blindness. As Root writes, "In the modern era our attention has been drawn away from what our ancestors thought was obvious: that a personal God acts and moves in the world. Some would say this movement represents liberation: we've put aside an untenable belief. . . . [Instead, what] we've acquired [is] a unique observation blindness. It's not that we've given up an untenable belief but that [our secular age has] drawn our attention away from divine action and toward something else. New forms of attention make us unable to see what was once obvious." We think religion is a matter of *belief*. Root points out that something deeper and more fundamental is going on. Faith is a matter of *perception*. Faith isn't forcing yourself to believe in unbelievable things; faith is *overcoming attentional blindness*. Phrased differently, faith is about *enchantment* or, rather, a re-enchantment: the intentional recovery of a holy capacity to see and experience God in the world. Without this ability, pervasive cultural disenchantment erodes our faith, and we're seeing the effects all around us, in our homes, in pews, and in the culture at large.

How enchantment flows out of perceptual *intention* and *attention* is wonderfully illustrated in Exodus in the story of Moses and the burning bush. After his flight from Egypt, Moses is tending his father-in-law's sheep in the middle of the desert near Mount Horeb. There, in the middle of nowhere, he catches sight of a bush that's caught fire. Strangely, the bush isn't being burnt up. Intrigued and fascinated, Moses says, "I must turn aside and see this strange sight."

I must turn aside. This is the key point. Encountering God's presence requires a shift of attention. Moses must *intentionally direct his attention* to behold the strange sight.

We must as well in this skeptical age. God is there, but we're going to have to retrain ourselves to see. I like how Marilynne Robinson describes this in her novel *Gilead*: "It has seemed to me sometimes as though the Lord breathes on this poor gray ember of Creation and it turns to radiance—for a moment or a year or the span of a life. And then it sinks back into itself again, and to look at it no one would know it had anything to do with fire, or light. . . . Wherever you turn your eyes the world can shine like transfiguration. You don't have to bring a thing to it except a little willingness to see." Enchantment starts with this willingness to see. As the Christian mystic Simone Weil said, "Attention is the only faculty of the soul that gives access to God." Disenchantment isn't about disbelief. Disenchantment is a failure to *attend*.

As a college professor at a Christian university, I witness the effects of disenchantment up close in my classrooms. Most of my students think—and likely you do as well—that the entire point of being a Christian is to "be a good person." My progressive and conservative students each have their own visions about what this "good person" should look like. Regardless, when faith is reduced to moral or political performance, life with God is stripped of its strange, startling, sacred magic. Faith becomes being a good neighbor and voting well. And I don't disagree; being a good person is a huge part of following Jesus, and I'm even comfortable saying it's the most important part. But more is required to sustain our vision of goodness decade after decade, especially when the work becomes costly and inconvenient or when we face failure and disillusionment. Beyond goodness, there is also the pressing problem that morality and politics do not heal the deep pain we're experiencing in the modern world. Anxiety, depression, addiction, loneliness, and suicide are all on the rise. My students are very good people. They are kind, tolerant, environmentally conscientious, and justice-minded. But they are also very unhappy, anxious, and lonely. Something in this skeptical age is hurting them. And not just them. We're all feeling lost and unwell.

I call this the Ache, and I spend time with my students, as I will with you, mapping the contours of this pain. The Ache is the photographic negative of enchantment, the hole that's been left in our lives because we've turned our attention away from God. The Ache is our disenchantment with disenchantment, our doubts about our doubts, our skepticism about being so skeptical. Perhaps paradoxically, exploring the Ache is often the first step back toward enchantment. It's like a doctor testing an injured limb, moving it tentatively and asking, "Does this hurt?" We'll do the same as we walk across the landscape of disenchantment asking, "Does this hurt?" Because disenchantment does hurt. Something we need is missing from our lives. And we're feeling the pain.

What's missing is enchantment. For my students, disenchantment reduces their faith to morality or political action. But morality and politics don't heal the Ache, not fully or completely. An enchanted faith is, by contrast, a wonder- and joy-filled adventure with God, opening the wardrobe door and finding yourself in Narnia. As Anne Lamott says, our prayers keep bumping into three big words: *Thanks*, *Help*, and *Wow*. These three words are prayers of enchantment, expressions of gratitude, dependence, and hope. This is the magic that sustains and empowers our moral and political efforts across our life span. This is the enchantment that begins to heal the Ache. Faith is more than moral self-improvement and election-year drama. Faith is a romance, a meeting with, in the words of Dante, "the Love that moves the sun and the other stars." Our moral alignment with this Love is, of course, a huge part of the story. But it's the burning bush encounter with God that vitalizes, animates, excites, and sustains our faith. True, these experiences may be fleeting and elusive, isolated and unpredictable—like thunderclaps in a long, dark night—but they form the bedrock of Christian life. Ask anyone who has carried their faith over many decades about how they have done so. They have not been forcing themselves to believe in unbelievable things. Rather, the doggedly faithful will share stories about burning bush moments in their lives when they bumped into God, encountered a Love and Mystery beyond words and descriptions. These "strange sights" are not flights of fantasy or wishful thinking. They are the most reality-filled moments of our lives, the truest things we have ever experienced. These mystical encounters, as rare as they may be, are the foundations of faith.

Sometimes these moments are dramatic and clear, like Paul's encounter with Jesus on the road to Damascus. But for myself and many others, these enchanted moments have been more soft, quiet, and subtle. I have never heard the voice of God speaking audibly to me or seen a vision, but I have seen the world shine like transfiguration. I've had experiences like the one that transformed the life of the Catholic monk and writer Thomas Merton. On March 18, 1958, Merton was in Louisville, Kentucky, for an appointment. He was standing on the corner of Fourth and Walnut, looking at all the busy people bustling around him, shopping and working. And there, standing on that busy corner, enchantment happened. God breathes on the gray ember of the world, and it glows. Merton shared what he saw that day:

In Louisville, at the corner of Fourth and Walnut, in the center of the shopping district, I was suddenly overwhelmed with the realization that I loved all those people, that they were mine and I theirs, that we could not be alien to one another even though we were total strangers. It was like waking from a dream. . . .

This sense of liberation from an illusory difference was such a relief and such a joy to me that I almost laughed out loud. . . . I have the immense joy of being man, a member of a race in which God Himself became incarnate. As if the sorrows and stupidities of the human condition could overwhelm me, now I realize what we all are. And if only everybody could realize this! But it cannot be explained. There is no way of telling people that they are all walking around shining like the sun.

On that busy street corner, Merton saw the "strange sight." He didn't hear the voice of God from the sky or see a vision of angels. He saw the world shine like transfiguration. That is what enchantment has felt like for me. Enchantment hasn't been the supernatural vision but the surprising rush of joy and love—enjoying the gift of a sunrise, bearing witness to a small act of kindness, watching the breeze dancing in the branches of a tree, or seeing the person standing right in front of you shining like the sun. I've seen the world, if only briefly and in my peripheral vision, light up with fire. I expect you have as well. The big encouragement I have for all of us living in this skeptical age is simply this: more. Let's open our eyes to see more.

Before moving on to the good stuff, let's pause to address three possible questions or objections that you might be having right here at the start.

First, why resort to fancy, unfamiliar terms like *enchantment* and *disenchantment* when it would be much simpler to speak of *belief* versus *disbelief*? Because isn't that what we're really talking about?

Actually, no, we're not. The issue is the difference between *belief* and *experience*. Belief is intellectual assent and agreement with the doctrinal propositions of faith. Experience exists prior to and drives belief. Experience gives birth to belief. It's hard to "believe" in God if belief isn't naming something in our lives, something we've felt, sensed, seen, or intuited. As the Christian mystical tradition teaches us, life with God is more about knowing than believing. The mystics didn't *believe* in God; they *encountered* God.

So it's crazy to demand or expect beliefs from people (or ourselves) where there is no experience. Without an experience of God, belief has no content, no reference, no object. No way to get to "Yes!" Demanding belief without experience is asking people to believe in nothing, for the word *God* would be hanging in thin air, pointing to a gaping hole in a person's life. Belief without experience is an empty bucket, making it a very useless, discardable thing. But if there's water in the bucket, if our beliefs are carrying precious experiences of Thanks, Help, and Wow, well, you're going to hold onto that bucket for fear of spilling the water, especially if you're standing in the middle of a disenchanted desert dying of thirst. I'd like us to spend less time talking about the bucket and start filling it with water.

A second question you might be asking is, Are we really as disenchanted as I've been making it out? People still believe in strange, supernatural stuff. It could be that we're not growing more disenchanted but that we're undergoing a *change* in enchantments. For example, Stephen Asma describes modern supernatural beliefs in his book *Why We Need Religion*. Asma notes that his sophisticated university students frequently scoff at the view of science they see displayed in the many creationist museums sprinkled across America, each devoted to preaching a literal reading of Genesis against the reigning

scientific consensus. In their dismissal of a literal reading of the Bible's creation story, Asma's students seem to
be perfect examples of modern, secular disenchantment.
Science rules! But that's not quite the case, as Asma goes
on to observe:

> But now it gets interesting. My students believe
> in ghosts.
>
> It's not just a few students, or an odd cohort,
> that believe in ghosts. It's a vast majority. Over
> the last decade I have informally polled my stu-
> dents and discovered that around 80 percent of
> them believe in ghosts. . . .
>
> If you are surprised to find such a high num-
> ber of ghost believers, you might also be alarmed
> to discover that almost half of my students also
> believe in astrology. . . .
>
> Much has been made recently of the non-
> religious nature of the Millennials, given that
> they self-identify as "unaffiliated" when polls ask
> them about religion. They are indeed disaffected
> about organized institutional religion, but we
> would be mistaken if we read this as an Enlight-
> enment style triumph of scientific literacy. They
> are devoted to mysticism, supernaturalism, [and]
> pseudoscience . . . and the same [students] who
> think the idea of heaven and hell is ridiculous, see
> karma and reincarnation as manifestly obvious.

Maybe we aren't as disenchanted as we appear to be. Some have called this "the myth of disenchantment," arguing that modern people are as enchanted as they have always been. I don't think it's quite that simple. Disenchantment isn't a myth; it's a huge and growing force in Europe and America. Magic-eel tourism has been on the decline for quite a while now. But it is true that the spiritual landscape is complicated and diverse. Disenchantment has been on the rise for the last five hundred years, but as Asma's students illustrate, enchantment remains a powerful force. Consequently, what is often taken as evidence for disenchantment might actually be a shifting of enchantments. We can describe this shift as a movement away from a *religious* enchantment toward a *spiritual* enchantment, creating the growing "spiritual but not religious" phenomenon. By *religious enchantment*, I mean an encounter with sacred transcendence, God existing outside, above, and beyond the cosmos. By *spiritual enchantment*, I mean—as Steven Smith describes in his book *Pagans and Christians in the City*—an immanent encounter with the sacred, the divine located *within* creation itself. For our conversation, disenchantment names both the rise of unbelief generally along with a movement away from a religious enchantment, an encounter with a transcendent Creator.

Which brings us to a final concern: obviously, there isn't one type of enchantment. There are enchantments that Christians should be worried about and avoid. So when we speak of re-enchanting faith, we need to attend to the potential for misenchantment. For example, whenever I, as a psychologist, discuss the importance of experience in our faith, my theologian friends light their hair on fire. The fear is that if we lean too heavily on our experiences, our faith will be blown about by our whims and fancies. And that's absolutely true; experience must be checked or all sorts of bad things can happen. We need to discern the spirits and heed the exhortation of 1 John 4:1: "Beloved, do not believe every spirit, but test the spirits to see whether they are from God." You and I will kick the tires of the various enchantments on offer in the world in order to separate God's enchantment from the kooky, the dangerous, and the self-indulgent.

Preliminaries now out of the way, let me say I think Thomas Merton got it exactly right. God is everywhere and in everything, and we cannot be without Him. It's simply impossible. But we have some vision problems. So join me on a journey to re-enchant our faith in this skeptical age. Let's turn aside to see the strange sights. Burning like transfiguration, the world is full of fire and light. God is there, right in front of you, dancing.

All you need to do is bring a little willingness to see.

PART 1

ATTENTION BLINDNESS

1

THE SLOW DEATH
OF GOD

"In U.S., Decline of Christianity Continues at Rapid Pace"—so blared the headline of a report released by the Pew Research Center in October of 2019. Buried in the report was a shocking revelation: According to Pew, in 2019, 84 percent of the silent generation (those born between 1928 and 1945) identified as Christians. So did 76 percent of the baby boomers (born between 1946 and 1964). But less than half of the millennial generation (those born in the 1980s and 1990s) identified as Christian (49 percent), while 40 percent of millennials identified as "nothing in particular" (the religious "nones").

This is a wake-up call for the church. For the first time in the history of the United States, there is a generation the *majority* of whom don't identify as Christian. And these generational trends are just one part of the larger story in the United States concerning the decline of Christianity and religious belief. For example, in 2019, Americans who described their religious identity as atheist, agnostic, or "nothing in particular" increased to 26 percent of the total population, up from 17 percent in 2009. And these rates of unbelief are accelerating with each successive generation.

"God is dead," declared the philosopher Friedrich Nietzsche. I don't think God is dead yet, but God is most definitely on life support.

I want to tell you the story about the slow death of God in the West, how a world once filled with magic and miracles became disbelieving and doubting. It is a story with some surprising twists and turns. While sad, this is a story you need to hear. Somehow, somewhere, we lost our way. Let's stop, retrace our steps, and figure out where we made the wrong turns.

As I've shared, five hundred years ago, we lived in an enchanted world. The existence of God was taken for granted. *Of course* God existed. There was a heaven and there was a hell, and everything you did pointed you toward one destination or the other. Five hundred years ago, in the words of 1 Peter 5, the devil prowled the world like a hungry lion, seeking souls to tempt and devour. If not the devil, then his minions, the hordes of demons that would afflict, injure, trick, tempt, lure, harm, and even possess hapless humans. But the faithful were not defenseless. Angels guarded and protected, along with the saints in heaven. Prayers petitioned divine aid and assistance. Visions and heavenly visitations gave guidance, support, and protection. Miracles were the norm and supernatural wonders abounded. On the edges of Christianity, and bleeding into it in ways that made them impossible to separate, were the enchantments of the pagan world. Life was filled with spells, curses, talismans, potions, magic, and superstitions. There were witches, ghosts, and creatures that haunted the night.

But that's not our world. Our world is disenchanted. Science has replaced superstition. To be sure, religious belief hasn't vanished, and the world remains supernatural and spooky in many ways. But people today do regularly doubt the existence of God, and rates of atheism and agnosticism continue to climb. We demand hard facts, data, and evidence. We revel in skepticism. Nothing is true for us until a scientist shows up. And for good reason: the gifts of modern medicine and technology are life giving and awe inspiring. The ancients thought the earth was flat. We've put a man on the moon.

True, disenchantment hasn't wholly won the day. Many of us, Christian and non-Christian, still move and live in an enchanted world. But something dramatic has changed over the last five hundred years in the West, especially in our relationship to God. We live in a secular, technological world that has pushed God and the supernatural to the margins. Things our ancestors took as manifestly obvious we now reject. A perceptual shift has occurred, one that has affected our ability to see and experience the "strange sights" all around us.

Let's explore how this perceptual shift occurred and why the world became disenchanted. There's no single reason behind God's slow death, no single cause, but we can point to two important developments in the story.

Go back to the Pew report concerning the decline of religious belief in America. If you took a poll among your friends and coworkers about what's driving the trends, I bet you'd get a one-word answer: science.

We assume that science and faith are enemies and that the rise of science has pushed God out of the world. Unfortunately, many Christians have contributed to this impression. Ever since the infamous Scopes Monkey Trial in 1925, where biblical fundamentalism squared off with Darwinian evolution in a courtroom in Dayton, Tennessee, we've seen Christians go to war with the reigning scientific consensus, from evolution to climate change.

But while science has been a part of the slow death of God, we shouldn't blame science for disenchantment. Many scientists happily believe in God, and rates of religious belief are often higher in university science departments than in other academic disciplines. True, biblical fundamentalists reject things like evolution, but the Catholic Church, the largest Christian denomination in the world, is quite comfortable with Charles Darwin. And let's not forget that many of the figures who launched the Scientific Revolution were deeply religious. If the Scientific Revolution began with an apple falling from a tree and hitting Sir Isaac Newton on the head, let's also remember that Newton spent a lot of time looking for hidden prophecies in the Bible. Clearly, Newton saw no contradiction in believing in both God and gravity.

But something did change when that apple hit Sir Isaac on the head. It wasn't science exactly; it was how Newton's law of gravity and laws of motion altered how we *imagined* and *experienced* the world. Facts have never been a threat to faith—the more facts, the merrier!—but science changed our *vision*, how we beheld and perceived the world. This is the first big surprise in our story.

Imagine walking along a beach and finding a vintage pocket watch. You wind the watch and observe the hands as they begin to move. You open the back of the watch and examine the intricate latticework of gears moving in synchrony. Contemplating the complex design of the watch, you ask the obvious question: Who made this? Obviously, some intelligent mind crafted this object. Where there is a watch, there must be a watchmaker.

You've likely heard this argument before, used as a proof for the existence of God. We call it the "argument from design." The created world is like a complicated watch, displaying intricate design and order. Such order, it is argued, could not have come about through random, chaotic processes. The design and order of the world display evidence of an Intelligent Designer. A watch implies a Watchmaker.

The argument from design has been a staple of Christian apologetics for generations. Many have found it persuasive. Perhaps you do as well. But for our story, I don't really care if you find the argument from design convincing. What I want you to observe is how the argument from design played a huge role in disenchanting the world. Yes, you heard me correctly: an argument for the existence of God helped bring about the slow death of God.

To see this, let's go back to Sir Isaac and the apple. Newton's discovery of the law of gravity was a critical development in what we call Newtonian mechanics, the laws of gravity and motion that govern the dynamic interactions of physical objects in the world, their movements and collisions. While facts are never antagonistic to faith, Newtonian mechanics did change how we imagined the cosmos. Before Newton, objects moved in consistent, regular patterns because they were obeying the benevolent will of God. In the final lines of *The Divine Comedy*, Dante stands looking into the heavens to behold "the Love that moves the sun and the other stars." Before Newton's apple, Love moved the stars. But after Newton's apple, this changed. In light of Newtonian mechanics, we came to view the cosmos as a *machine*, less alive and more like an intricately designed watch.

Seeing nature as a machine was a huge perceptual shift. Watches imply watchmakers, but once wound, the watch doesn't need the watchmaker anymore. The watch runs *on its own*, thank you very much, *independently* of the watchmaker. Watches don't obey the Love that moves the stars. Watches tick because they obey the laws of physics.

The world was once alive and enchanted, quivering with the love of God. The mere existence of the world was a miracle, the gift of each new morning inspiring awe, reverence, and gratitude. We've lost track of that miracle. We don't behold the world as crackling with God's power and love. We study the Machine in our science classes. Sure, perhaps at the start, with the big bang, God kicked the whole thing off. But once it got ticking, the cosmos no longer needed God. The laws of physics took over. We sidelined the Love that moves the stars, and God began to die his slow death.

In 1517, Martin Luther nailed his Ninety-Five Theses to the church doors in Wittenberg, Germany. With that act of defiance, the Protestant Reformation began. I am a proud Protestant, but the second big surprise in our story is how the Protestant Reformation played a significant role in disenchanting the world. This impact should be obvious if you've had any experience with the Catholic tradition.

When I was in the sixth grade, my parents enrolled me in Blessed Sacrament, a Catholic grade school in our hometown. Blessed Sacrament was a huge culture shock. I was a proud member of the Churches of Christ, a Bible-thumping, Protestant denomination. Plopping into the middle of Catholicism was very disorienting. I'd never been to Mass before, never faced the enchantments of the Catholic faith. Suddenly, I found myself surrounded by holy water, nuns, priests, rosaries, the sign of the cross, kneeling, incense, liturgy, saints, stained glass, and statues. I still remember the trauma of my first Ash Wednesday at Blessed Sacrament. I'd accidentally seated myself on the first row on the aisle. When the priest stepped forward for the imposition of the ashes, he gestured for me to rise and come forward. I was first in line, but he didn't know I was a confused Protestant kid. I hesitated, and he gestured more forcefully. Under his gaze and feeling my neighbor nudge me to get up, I found myself standing. I walked forward toward the priest, wondering what he was going to do to me. He rubbed something on my head, said some words I didn't pick up in my confusion, and gestured for me to go back to my seat. The flustered priest probably assumed I was a bad Catholic when in fact I was a disoriented Protestant kid who was accidentally forced to participate in the ritual. I went back to my seat, puzzling over what had been rubbed onto my forehead. Soon I observed the black crosses on the foreheads of my classmates as they returned to their seats. Stunned, I was convinced I'd just participated in some dark, occult ritual. I couldn't get to the bathroom fast enough to wipe the black mark off my forehead.

(Let me confess, to all my Catholic readers and friends, that I look back with bemusement upon that traumatized Church of Christ kid. Today, I adore Ash Wednesday. It's one of my favorite days of the liturgical year.)

As I learned on my first Ash Wednesday, the Catholic experience is very enchanted. Ashes and holy water are infused with sacred significance. The Eucharist itself is a miracle. In fact, one of the concerns we Protestants have about Catholics is that their faith is *too* enchanted, too magical and superstitious. Praying to St. Anthony—patron saint of lost things—to help you find your misplaced car keys strikes many Protestants as akin to worrying about black cats crossing your path. As we'll see, in moving away from the enchanted world of Catholicism, the Protestant Reformation kicked off a variety of developments within Christianity that played a significant role in disenchanting the world.

To illustrate this, consider how some developments within Protestantism disenchanted space, time, people, and the church:

Think about passing a Catholic church on a city street. Wanting a moment of peace from the hustle and bustle of modern life—the traffic noises, the people rushing past—you stop and enter the church. The first thing you'd notice is that the doors are open, as they are in most Catholic churches during the day. "This is a sanctuary," the open doors communicate. "Come inside."

You enter and are instantaneously transported to an enchanted world. You catch the smell of frankincense. The sunlight is filtered through a kaleidoscope of stained glass. Candles twinkle. Statues and artwork surround you. Everything you see and smell, along with the quietness, informs you that this is a sacred, magical place. You're standing on holy ground. You've walked through the wardrobe door and found yourself in Narnia. Even nonbelievers feel a difference when they enter a Catholic cathedral. A hushed, reverent stillness overtakes you.

Now think of an evangelical worship auditorium. If you tried to enter the auditorium of my church during the week, the first thing you'd notice is that the doors are locked. Our auditorium isn't a sanctuary where stray pilgrims come to encounter God. Even if you were able to enter the auditorium, you wouldn't find much there that would remind you of God. There would be lots of chairs, music stands, cords for instruments, and a drum kit off to the side. We don't seek out these sorts of spaces for prayer or contemplation. We look for more enchanted spaces than large, empty auditoriums.

There's a beautiful idea behind this utilitarian approach toward worship spaces. As good Protestants will tell you, God isn't restricted to a place. We don't "go to church" because God is found in a building. God is everywhere. The bland, functional evangelical worship auditorium clearly sends that message: This is just an ordinary room; there's nothing special or magical about it. God is with and goes with God's people. So when we leave the building, it's OK to lock the doors, because God doesn't remain behind waiting for us to return next Sunday. God is out in the world, and we leave the building to encounter God in our daily lives.

That is some profound and beautiful theology, and it explains why many Protestants elect not to enchant their spaces the way Catholics do. God is everywhere, so there's no need to associate God with a particular space, like a church or cathedral. All places are equally sacred and holy.

But while that's surely true, it also presents some challenges. Specifically, enchantment thrives when it is made visible, when we set some places apart, treating them as sacred, unique, and particular locations where God is encountered. While God is everywhere, without visible and visual reminders of God's presence, we're going to struggle in our disenchanted age to remember that God is even there at all. When faith is a matter of *attention*, we need visual cues to capture and captivate our hearts and minds. Catholics get this; Protestants, by and large, not so much. Without visual nudges, our attention is pulled in a million different directions, and we find, at the end of a long, busy workday, that we've hardly thought of God at all. The world is shining like transfiguration, but we're too hurried and distracted to see it.

Beyond space, think about how we keep track of time.

Let me ask you a question: What time is it? What season of the year is it?

The answers we give are predictable. It's 3:15 p.m. It's Monday. It's summertime, a few weeks before the Fourth of July.

Now let's think about how time was kept five hundred years ago.

What time is it?

It's Lauds.

It's Lent, two weeks before Easter.

Time used to be sacred. The day wasn't marked by the company timeclock but with church bells and a cycle of daily prayer, called the Liturgy of the Hours. Days weren't measured by "working nine to five"; they were marked by prayers offered at fixed times throughout the day:

- Vigil (said at around 2 a.m.)
- Lauds (said at dawn)
- Prime (said during the "First Hour," around 6 a.m.)
- Terce (said during the "Third Hour," around 9 a.m.)
- Sext (said during the "Sixth Hour," around noon)
- None (said during the "Ninth Hour," around 3 p.m.)
- Vespers (said "at the lighting of the lamps," about 6 p.m.)
- Compline (said before going to bed, around 7 p.m.)

Catholic monastics still pray the Liturgy of the Hours, as do many laypeople. My personal prayer habit is to pray Lauds (morning prayer) and Vespers (evening prayer).

Beyond the Liturgy of the Hours, time was also enchanted by the liturgical calendar, the yearlong cycle of holy days and seasons governing the worship and celebrations of the church, like Christmas and Easter. You've probably also heard of Advent, Epiphany, Lent, Ash Wednesday, Holy Week, Palm Sunday, Maundy Thursday, Good Friday, and Pentecost.

These feasts, seasons, holy days, and celebrations of the liturgical year were how we kept time five hundred years ago. *Liturgical* time was *enchanted* time. It still is. Christmas remains magical, even in our disenchanted age. But even Christmas is struggling to hold its own against the rising tide of disenchantment. Our "holy days" have been reduced to "holidays," time off granted by employers rather than seasons hallowed by our faith. Time has become disenchanted, stripped of its sacred magic. No one needs God anymore to know what time it is.

Here's another question for you: What does it mean to be a saint?

Catholics and Protestants have two very different answers to this question. For Catholics, saints are enchanted persons. Literally. For a person to be canonized as a saint in the Catholic Church, at least two miracles have to be attributed to them. Catholics also pray to saints for help and protection. That's about as enchanted as you can get. For Protestants, the situation is quite different: every Christian is a saint. Sainthood isn't an aspiration, restricted to a special few, but the birthright of every believer. In Protestantism, sainthood is disenchanted, more about your status as being saved than about your exemplary holiness or any miraculous deeds you might have done. There are deep and important reasons why Protestantism applies the word *saint* to each and every believer, but it's also true that when everyone is a saint, no one is a saint. Protestants are very reluctant to elevate and distinguish anyone from among their group as being particularly exemplary or holy, as being a saint among the saints. In Protestantism, exemplary Christians are not considered to be a human "thin space," a person whose humility, gentleness, goodness, joy, peace, kindness, and love bring us into closer contact with God. *Saint* no longer names a deep mystical union with God but becomes a synonym for *believer*, even if that believer is a toxic, harmful, and selfish person. And where toxic, harmful people are called saints, the label *saint* is going to lose some of its mystical, enchanted luster.

If you're a Christian, I assume you've taken the Lord's Supper, also called Communion or the Eucharist. We observe the Lord's Supper all sorts of ways. Maybe you take it at your church every Sunday, or perhaps a few times a year. Maybe you use wine where others use grape juice. Maybe you come down to the altar to sip out of a chalice, or maybe you pass trays with little plastic cups.

Christians celebrate the Lord's Supper in all sorts of ways. But here's another question: What happens during the Lord's Supper? Specifically, during the Lord's Supper, does anything particularly *supernatural* or *miraculous* happen to the bread and wine? Protestants and Catholics have very different answers to this question.

By and large, Protestants don't think anything miraculous or supernatural happens to the bread and wine in the Lord's Supper. The "elements" of Communion remain exactly what they are, bread and wine. The physical "substance" of the bread and wine undergoes no supernatural change to become something different. In my tradition, the bread and wine are merely memory aids, objects we use to bring the sacrifice of Jesus to mind. Some Protestants do believe that God is especially and particularly present in the Lord's Supper, that there is a grace we experience in eating the bread and drinking the wine that occurs nowhere else. But either way, the bread remains bread and the wine remains wine.

For Catholics, the situation is completely different. According to the Catholic doctrine of transubstantiation, during the Eucharist, the physical bread and wine are miraculously and supernaturally changed into the actual—really and truly!—body and blood of Jesus Christ. In the Eucharist, Jesus becomes physically and literally present in the room. Whenever I try to explain transubstantiation to my Protestant college students, looks of confusion appear on their faces. It's hard for Protestants to wrap their heads around what happens in the Catholic Mass. "Whenever you go to Mass," I tell my students, "you are witnessing a miracle."

We can debate all this, the Protestant versus the Catholic views of what happens to the bread and wine during Communion. But what we can all agree on is that Catholics have the more enchanted view of the sacrament. For Protestants, the Lord's Supper is mostly about *memory*; for Catholics, it's about a *miracle*.

That represents a huge change in how we think about the purpose of going to church. In fact, without the miracle, most evangelicals elect to skip the Lord's Supper on Sundays. The central, focal enchantment that once gathered the church has gone missing.

Space, time, people, and church—in every instance, we've seen how various developments within Protestantism shifted away from the more enchanted Catholic experience. And while these theological impulses within Protestantism are praiseworthy, defensible, and valuable—I'm not arguing that you should convert to Catholicism—the Protestant experience nudged the West away from enchantment.

In many ways, Protestantism has been a journey from the *mystical* to the *moral*. This *mystical-to-moral shift* has played a significant role in disenchanting the world. I think it's had a bigger impact on faith than the Scientific Revolution. If God is slowly dying, it's because Christians stopped seeking God and started to focus on being *good*.

Protestantism introduced a moralism and puritanism that was largely absent in the Catholic experience. You see this contrast even today. When I attended Blessed Sacrament, I remember how shocked I was when I saw a priest smoking. And Catholics love to quote the line from Hilaire Belloc, who quipped, "Wherever the Catholic sun doth shine, there's always laughter and good red wine." Such sentiments offended my moralistic Protestant upbringing, where I was told that Christians shouldn't drink alcohol. Protestants have routinely suspected that their Catholic brothers and sisters were morally lax. When I later attended Mercyhurst Prep, a Catholic high school, weekly confession looked suspiciously like a "get out of jail free" card for my partying Catholic friends.

The pietistic, social reforming impulse within Protestantism appeared very early in John Calvin's Geneva, where the civic Christian authorities took a meddling interest in the moral habits of their neighbors, their carousing, drinking, smoking, lewd language, and sexual promiscuity. When the citizens of Geneva asked Calvin to take charge of the town, his response set the tone for the moralistic vibe that has come to characterize Protestantism. "If you desire to have me as your pastor," Calvin ominously intoned to the city officials, "then you will have to correct the disorder of your lives." This moralizing impulse was especially felt in America, settled as it was by Puritans. Anyone raised in a conservative Protestant home has experienced firsthand this pietistic emphasis on personal holiness. Good Christians do not swear, drink, use drugs, smoke, or have sex before marriage, along with other sins that get added to the list: avoiding R-rated movies, no dancing, refusing to listen to "worldly" music, dressing modestly, and avoiding *Harry Potter*. To be fair, Protestantism has also focused on reforming evil social arrangements. The socially conscious piety of evangelicals like William Wilberforce played a key role in the English abolitionist movement, as it would later in America. Participating in benevolence, charity, and justice ministries has played and continues to play an influential part in the Protestant pursuit of holiness and piety.

Holiness and social justice also play a vital role in Catholicism. The social teachings of the Catholic Church are a beacon of light I wish more Protestants knew about. But ground zero of the Catholic faith has always been the miracle of the Mass. Protestantism displaced this central, daily miracle and replaced it with piety, purity, holiness, morality, and "doing good." Much of this moral performance is captured by "the Protestant work ethic": being an honest, thrifty, hardworking, morally upright, charitable, and tax-paying citizen. And wherever Protestants are found on the liberal, progressive, Democratic side of the political aisle, "being a good person" looks like social justice and environmental activism. For Protestants, liberal or conservative, morality and politics are central and on the front burner. Encountering God is increasingly an afterthought, if it is thought of at all.

Of course, Catholics haven't been immune to this mystical-to-moral shift. Whenever you see the purpose of going to Mass called into question among skeptical Catholics, when the central miracle is doubted, you'll observe the same moralization and politicization of their faith. Where being a good person is enough, the Mass becomes irrelevant and discardable.

All of this, the moralization and politicization of faith, leads to the slow death of God. Here's how it happens. When the Christian experience shifts away from the mystical toward "being a good person," the foundation of faith is relocated and placed in a very vulnerable location, like a cup set dangerously close to the edge of the table or a rock pushed to the edge of a cliff. Why? Because you don't have to believe in God to be a good person. There are many people who don't believe in God who are amazing, generous, and loving people. And once you make that observation, that you don't need God to be good, the whole reason many of us have for believing in God simply evaporates. The glass falls off the table and shatters, and the rock tips over into the abyss.

If you think my analysis is wrong or overstated, I suggest you have a conversation with some young people, those millennials and Gen Zers who are leaving the faith. If you ask them, the younger generations in our pews generally assume that the entire point of being a Christian is to "be like Jesus," which is Christian speak for "being a good person." As I've said, my conservative and progressive students have very different visions of what "being like Jesus" looks like. But either way, they equate Christianity with their moral and political performance. And once this move is made, once Christianity is reduced to moral hygiene or social justice, it's just a short hop to question the usefulness of rolling out of bed on a Sunday morning to go to church or the meaningfulness of believing in God.

Actually, the situation is a whole lot worse than what I've just described. For many millennials and Gen Zers, it's not that the church is irrelevant; the church is a part of the problem. Millennials and Gen Zers are more progressive than their parents and grandparents, more tolerant and inclusive on the issues of gender, race, and sexuality. So if the point of following Jesus is being a loving, tolerant person, then there's little attraction with a church they associate with sexism, racism, and homophobia.

Stepping back, you can see how all this affects faith in our skeptical age. When the experience of Christianity shifts from the mystical to the moral—illustrated in Calvin's Geneva, the Protestant work ethic, and the social justice activism of the younger generations—it becomes easier to question and then jettison both God and the church. Since atheists can be loving people and social justice warriors, it doesn't seem to matter much if you believe in God or not. If you don't need God to be good, then God is useless.

This is the sad, surprising story about the slow death of God in the West, the story of how our world became disenchanted. Two good and well-intentioned developments within Christianity ended up killing God. When the world became a machine, God was deemed irrelevant to its day-to-day operations. And when being a good person became the goal of faith, it became clear that you didn't need either God or the church to be good.

These two things—seeing the world as a *machine* and reducing Christianity to *morality*—disenchanted the world. Each in their own way made God distant and unnecessary. Slowly, our vision shifted. The miracles staring us in the face faded from our view.

This is a disappointing story, but I'm not sharing it to depress you. I want us to see where we made two wrong turns so that we can learn to re-enchant our faith in this skeptical age. If viewing the cosmos as a machine disenchanted us, we can work to recover the vision of Gerard Manley Hopkins, who saw that "the world is charged with the grandeur of God." Likewise, if reducing Christianity to moral and political performance disenchanted us, we can cultivate and recover a more mystical approach to faith while still trying to be good people. Our wrong turns are clues about where we need to do some work.

The story of God's slow death is sad, but the tale shows us exactly where we got turned around and what could be done to get ourselves back on the right track. Our vision might have shifted, but God never went any-where. The dancing gorilla is still right there in front of us.

2

WELCOME TO THE ACHE

"People don't have a desire for God anymore," said my dad.

Dad and I were on a golf course, talking as we do when golfing, about God, faith, and the church. Dad's been a leader in the small church I grew up in for as long as I can remember. We were talking about the demographic decline of churches, the disappearance of families and young people, congregations aging and graying. It's a scene playing out across America in our disenchanted, increasingly skeptical, post-Christian nation.

Squeezed between my errant golf shots, Dad felt he'd put his finger on the problem: a lack of desire for God, especially among the young. But I disagreed.

"I actually think young people do desire God," I shared while slicing another drive into the trees. "They just don't know it. They call this desire anxiety, depression, or loneliness. Everywhere you look in America, you see this longing for God. You see it in rising rates of suicide and addiction. People are in pain. But we've lost the ability to correctly name and diagnose the hurt. The only language young people have for God is the language of mental illness. When they say 'anxiety' or 'depression,' they are expressing a desire for God."

Speaking as a psychologist, I wasn't suggesting to my dad—or to you—that severe mental illness can be quickly fixed by "coming to Jesus." What I am pointing out is how very unwell we are as a society. The evidence is everywhere. As I've said, rates of suicide, anxiety, depression, loneliness, and addiction are all on the rise, especially among young people. So we have to ask, What's causing us so much pain? Why is there so much hurt? Why is everyone feeling so anxious, unsettled, and fragile in this skeptical age?

We're all searching for some answers to these questions. We know the familiar suspects. Social media. Political polarization. The economic struggles of the middle class. College debt. No doubt, these all play a role. But these are stressors rather than root causes. In medicine, there's a theory of illness called the "vulnerability-stress model." We become ill when a stressor intersects with a vulnerability. For example, heart disease might run in my family. That's an inherited vulnerability I have. But if I don't put stress on that vulnerability, I can avoid or reduce my risk of getting heart disease. I can exercise, eat well, watch my weight, and avoid smoking. But if I refuse to do these things—if I am sedentary, overweight, and a smoker—my risk of heart disease will increase. I'd be placing a lot of stress upon my vulnerability.

Social media, politics, and economic strain are *stressors* rather than *causes*. We'd be able to better handle these stressors if we were more healthy and resilient. But we're not healthy or resilient: we're vulnerable, struggling to cope, and our happiness and peace of mind are increasingly fragile.

Let's explore this vulnerability. I'd like us to get to the root of what is causing us so much pain. As I've shared, with my students I call it the Ache.

God may be dead, but we sure do miss him.

The Ache is the chalk outline around God's dead body, marking the space that God once occupied in our lives. God is dead, or dying a slow death, in our skeptical age, and the Ache traces the contours of the space that God once held in our hearts and minds. When we trace this outline, the words we use are *anxiety, depression, suicide, addiction, loneliness, meaninglessness, cynicism, hopelessness, irritation, angst, malaise,* and *boredom.* This is what it feels like when God is dead.

The Ache is our disenchantment with disenchantment, the unease and pain we feel without God in our lives. Yes, in this secular age, we're skeptical, doubting, suspicious, questioning, and cynical. But many of us are becoming increasingly skeptical about our skepticism, starting to doubt our doubts and question our questions, and getting a little cynical about being so cynical. We're growing disenchanted with disenchantment, disillusioned with a world devoid of mystery, magic, and enchantment. We're starting to suspect that the vision of a mechanical and deterministic cosmos given to us by science is a bit inhuman and even monstrous. We're thirsting for the adventure of enchantment instead of reducing the drama of our lives to the laws of physics—our loves, joys, dreams, and pains simply the collision of dumb particles in an indifferent and mindless universe.

The Ache is how we talk about God in our disenchanted age. Given how our attention has shifted, it's harder to speak of God directly. So we're reduced to tracing the chalk outline around the space where God has gone missing.

Mapping the contours of our pain, tracing the chalk outline of the Ache, is the first step back toward enchantment. Living as we are in a skeptical world, the journey back toward enchantment starts with a disenchantment about our disenchantment, cultivating a disillusionment with our doubts. Many of us, though, have learned to embrace our doubts so strongly that this may be hard for us, especially if we've used our doubts and questions to create an image of ourselves as courageous and bold seekers of truth. It will be difficult for some to face the fact that our doubts are hurting us. But if your entire life has been devoted to putting question marks next to everything—especially the things you hold most sacred—is it any wonder we're all feeling a bit fragile and anxious? I think it's time to question some of those question marks.

So let's take a tour of the Ache, noting four locations where we're disenchanted with disenchantment. Let me point out some of our dissatisfactions with life in a skeptical age. Of course, the existence of the Ache is no proof for the existence of God. But tracing the Ache does cultivate a restlessness, a desire and longing for God. A spiritual thirst. Evoking this thirst is the first step back toward enchantment. It might be hard for us to *believe* in God, but it's very obvious that we *desire* God. And that desire is a prayer and a cry for help.

"Life changing. Inspiring. Holy."

Our friend Mike used these words to describe the Armstrong Redwoods State Natural Preserve in Guerneville, California. My wife, Jana, and I were going to be visiting San Francisco for the first time and reached out to Mike for some recommendations for places to visit. At the top of his list was making a trip to see the redwoods. Walking among the trees would be life changing, inspiring, and holy.

And it was. It's not just the size of the trees, how wide the trunks are, and how they soar into the sky. It's also their age. Our hands ran across the bark of redwoods older than the United States. In their aged width and height, the trees silence and humble you. It was like walking through a cathedral created by the hand of God.

Even if you don't believe in God, it's hard not to feel the enchantment of a redwood forest. I suspect that most of us feel enchantment most keenly in nature—in forests, by oceans, and on mountains. We encounter the magic when we see the blaze of autumn foliage, walk beneath the canopy of stars, witness the glory of a sunset, and behold the delicacy of a flower. When immersed in the beauty of the natural world, even the most skeptical and disenchanted among us are tempted to suspect that there might be something "more" going on in this mysterious world.

But all around us, the forces of disenchantment tempt us to strip the world of its sacred, mystical character. Disenchantment reduces the world to matter and chemistry, mere "stuff." Everything is just atoms, configured and reconfigured in different ways. There's nothing "magical" about the elements of the periodic table. The world is simply a collection of Lego blocks set in different arrangements. And while this description of physical reality might be fine for a science class, something in us resists reducing a redwood forest to organic chemistry. The enchantments of the natural world defy a wholly material and scientific description. Redwood forests are life changing, inspiring, and holy.

There's also something more sinister going on. When matter is reduced to interchangeable building blocks, a lump of raw material, it becomes very easy to commodify and commercialize, to exploit it for our own purposes. It's all just "stuff," after all, raw material, a collection of inert Lego blocks to be used and reused. Disenchant a redwood forest, strip it of its sacred magic, and you've got yourself a great source of lumber.

This is our first stop on our tour of the Ache. One of the easiest places to see and experience our disenchantment with disenchantment is in how we refuse to treat the natural world as a source of raw materials. This not only offends our enchanted feelings toward creation, but we also suspect that there is something diabolical going on, that disenchantment is necessary to facilitate the commercial exploitation of the planet. For human life to remain human, some things have to be preserved and cherished as holy and sacred, absolutely immune to commodification and exploitation. Many of us feel this most intensely when it comes to the natural world.

But our concerns here are not just about the natural world and redwood forests. We feel this tension with human beings as well.

There is a hypocrisy at the heart of secularism. A ghost haunts the machine of the modern world, a bit of magic that keeps the clockwork ticking. A ghost the skeptical pretend doesn't exist. Specifically, the moral vision of our disenchanted world is built upon a fundamental enchantment, the belief in the sacred worth of every human being. The moral foundation of the modern, secular world would collapse without this belief, the conviction that every human being is imbued with inestimable value and dignity. Our belief in universal human rights, the linchpin of secular morality, depends on this sacred recognition. Basically, human beings are like redwood trees. We cannot be reduced to raw material. We cannot be discarded and disposed of. Human beings are holy. The great hypocrisy of our skeptical age is that its greatest moral accomplishment—a moral vision founded upon universal human rights—depends on *enchantment*, a belief in the sacred character of human beings and life. No scientific equation or empirical test reveals this truth to us. The inviolate dignity of human persons doesn't show up in petri dishes, brain scans, or Hubble space photographs. Our shared belief in the sacred value of human beings is not a factual, empirical, testable, observable, data-driven claim. *Our dignity is an enchantment*, the ghost of God still haunting the machine, and it's the bit of supernaturalism that keeps the secular world from tipping into the moral abyss. And let's pray that this last flicker of magic never burns out, because if it ever does, you and I don't want to be around to see what happens next. Our belief in the sacred, inviolate worth of every human is an enchantment that's been smuggled into the modern world past the border guards of our doubts. And thank God this enchantment persists. Life would be inhuman without it.

As my friend Eve Poole points out, once upon a time, we used to have a word for the supernatural aspect of human beings. We called it the *soul*. In an age of brain scans and neuroscience, speaking of the soul seems outdated and antiquated, a bit of enchantment that we've learned to outgrow. But I bet if you asked your friends and neighbors if they have a soul, they all would answer yes. We still believe in the soul, even in this skeptical age. And we'd be horrified if anyone claimed otherwise. More and more people might doubt the existence of God, but God still haunts us. We crave the magic. We resist reducing our lives to biology. We are convinced that we are "more" than the sum total of our organs, bones, and tissues. Just like reducing redwood trees to lumber, there is something sociopathic about a purely scientific, materialistic description of human beings. When redwood trees lose their sacred magic, it becomes very easy to cut them down. And the same goes for human beings.

Prayer is hard in a skeptical age. Prayer can seem too much like magic, and we wonder if prayer even "works." (As consumers, we're always looking for a return on investment.) Yet atheists have shared with me how they pray sometimes and will say "I'll pray for you" when people share sorrows and pains with them. Praying atheists is a strange phenomenon, but the reason for it is quite simple. Everyone hallows.

Hallowing is an old word, but I love it. To hallow is to make or declare something as holy and sacred. I love the word because it points to a deeply human and universal activity. The reason we say "I'll pray for you," even if we don't believe in prayer or have serious doubts about the efficacy of prayer, is that when we face great pain, we feel compelled to hallow it, to set it apart from the normal stuff of daily life. And *hallowing* is *enchanting*. Disenchantment cannot hallow, and we feel its impotence acutely in the face of suffering. If a friend shares a deep sorrow with you, the words "I'll be thinking about you" or "I'm so sorry" seem woefully inadequate. So do "moments of silence" when we try to collectively hallow shared tragedy. When the pain is deep, we long for enchantment; we want to hallow the moment. We want to stand on holy ground, hand in hand. In a word, we want to *pray*. And we want others to pray for us. Even if we don't believe. So we pray.

When I face questions about prayer from my skeptical students, I always start with hallowing. I lead an adult Bible class every Sunday at my church. At the start of class, we take time to share prayer requests. The stories, concerns, worries, sorrows, and joys of the week pour out. More often than not, our prayer-request time gets pretty heavy. Cancer diagnoses, health problems, death, struggling marriages and families, job loss, and insecurity. After all our tears and anxieties mix together, I don't say, "Thanks for sharing, everyone. Good luck." No, I say, "Let's pray." And we pray. I don't expect magic from the prayer, I tell my students, nor can I answer all their questions about if prayer "works." But what I feel absolutely confident about is that *prayer is the only thing up to the task of hallowing* all that has been shared in our class. Prayer might not "work," but it hallows.

Prayer isn't the only example of this. We turn toward enchantment all the time. Everyone hallows. We hallow grief and loss with ceremony and ritual. Think of any funeral you've ever attended, how we reach for enchanted language, even if we don't believe it anymore. The famous atheist Christopher Hitchens once shared how moved he was by the reading of the King James Version of the Bible at his father's funeral. Nothing quite hallows a funeral like a reading from the King James Bible. Beyond funerals, places associated with tragedy or heroic sacrifice become holy shrines, sites of pilgrimage, enchanted spaces filled with vigils, flowers, and candles.

We also hallow the happy moments. Marriages are enchanted with solemn promises, rituals, fancy clothing, lights, and flowers. Clergy and churches are sought out to make the vows more sacred and weighty. We enchant birthdays with candles, singing, and "making a wish." Graduations are enchanted with the medieval, monastic robes and hats worn by faculty and students. Everywhere you turn, you bump into enchantment. Like I said, everyone hallows.

We hallow because human life requires a sacred texture. Some things have to be set apart from the common and ordinary flow of events. That's what hallowing means, after all—to "set apart" and "make holy." Mark Twain once said that history is just one damn thing after another. Perhaps, but we don't want our lives to become just one damn day after another. Some days need to be hallowed and set apart as special. Our lives demand texture and contrast. Some moments are ordinary, but others are special and noteworthy. We hallow these moments, often reaching for enchantments that we don't even believe in anymore. Even in our skeptical age, we keep saying, "I'll pray for you."

It is inhuman to live in a wholly disenchanted world. This is our second stop on our tour of the Ache. We need to give life a significance and weight beyond the next Netflix binge. We need our days to be more than scrolling through Twitter, Instagram, and Facebook. We crave holy days and sacred moments. We want ritual, holy shrines, and sacred pilgrimages. We need to light candles and sing. We want to hear the King James Bible read at our funerals. Because a *human* life is an *enchanted* life.

On October 19, 1944, Viktor Frankl and his wife, Tilly, were taken to Auschwitz. Frankl and his wife were Jews, and until the end of the war, Frankl lived in the Nazi death camps. Frankl was a psychiatrist, and he became a keen observer of camp life. After the war, Frankl's observations would eventually be published in the book *Man's Search for Meaning*.

If you surveyed psychologists and asked them to rank the greatest psychology books of all time, *Man's Search for Meaning* would probably come in at number one. At my school, we give the book as a gift to all our graduating seniors.

As you might expect, given its origin, *Man's Search for Meaning* is preoccupied with the question about how we can carry on in the face of suffering. And as the title of the book suggests, *meaning* is fundamental to this task. If our suffering is meaningless, we find the pain intolerable, and we cannot bear or carry it. But if our suffering is meaningful, if we can connect our pain to some purpose, we find the strength to carry on. The pain remains painful and just as heavy, but meaning gives us the strength to endure, to fight on, to keep going in the face of a new day. As Frankl succinctly said, "Those who have a 'why' to live, can bear with almost any 'how.'"

But meaning is very hard to secure in a disenchanted age. Even if we can secure meaning and purpose, our situation remains very provisional and fragile. This is our third stop on our tour of the Ache. As Frankl observed in the death camps and as anyone who has ever held the pieces of a broken dream in their hands can attest, life can rob you of meaning very quickly. Overnight, the story that gave your life direction, purpose, and value is destroyed. It's not a trip to Auschwitz, but it's a cancer diagnosis, a divorce, the death of a loved one, or the loss of a job. Yesterday you had one life, and today you awake to a totally different life, a life that has been robbed of what gave you meaning and purpose. Without that purpose, we don't know how to pick up the pieces. We don't know how to carry on.

If Frankl is right, and I think he is, that meaning is vital for mental health and well-being, we have to face the truth that meaning is fragile in our disenchanted age, which means that our mental health is going to be fragile as well. This is perhaps the biggest source driving the Ache. Without God, we have to construct meaning out of thin air, all on our own. We cobble together some reasons to get out of bed each morning, some excuse we tell ourselves to make our daily pains and struggles "meaningful." But we hardly believe what we're telling ourselves in this skeptical age. The cold, empty, indifferent cosmos doesn't care about our job stress or broken hearts. And even if we do convince ourselves that our lives "matter" in the midst of a silent, uncaring universe, the dreams that make our lives "matter" are prone to breaking. At a psychiatric hospital, I once helped treat a man who worked on an emergency response team. His job was, quite literally, saving lives. But after suffering a debilitating back injury, he was relegated to a desk job filling out paperwork. Not surprisingly, he was in our hospital being treated for suicidality and severe depression. And who could blame him? One injury and suddenly the thing that gave his life meaning—his job—was lost forever. Even if you are happy and fulfilled in your life today, we all know that what happened to this man could happen to any of us. Happiness is very, very fragile. After all, *happiness* is what *happens* to us. And what happens to us just isn't under our control.

It's no wonder we're all so anxious and depressed, no surprise that rates of addiction and suicide are on the rise. The meaning that is supposed to give our lives purpose is hard to locate, and even if we do find it, we know how fragile it can be, how quickly it can be taken away. Happiness in our skeptical age is skating on thin ice.

Given this fragile situation, psychologists have begun to study a variable called *mattering*. Mattering is, quite simply, the belief and conviction that you matter, that your life has cosmic significance regardless of external circumstances. As you might expect, given what Frankl has taught us, mattering is associated with psychological health and well-being. If you believe you matter, even in the face of failures and broken dreams, you're going to be more resilient in coping with the ups and downs of life.

But *mattering* is a form of *enchantment*, a conviction that, in some mystical way, the cosmos sees you and honors your pain and struggles. Your emotional and mental well-being rests upon this bit of magic. Because the conviction that you matter is nonsense when considered from a purely factual point of view. The physical universe, all those supernovas and black holes out there, cares nothing about your suffering or your heroic efforts to love and care for the people in your life. The belief that you matter is a residual bit of magic, similar to the soul, smuggled in from our enchanted past, the conviction that God sees and cares for you. This sentiment is beautifully captured by the old gospel hymn, composed by Civilla D. Martin, "His Eye Is on the Sparrow":

> *I sing because I'm happy,*
> *I sing because I'm free,*
> *for his eye is on the sparrow,*
> *and I know he watches me.*

The origin of "His Eye Is on the Sparrow" illustrates the profound impact an enchanted sense of mattering has upon our emotional health and psychological resiliency. As Civilla D. Martin recounted about the origin of her hymn,

> Early in the spring of 1905, my husband and I were sojourning in Elmira, New York. We contracted a

deep friendship for a couple by the name of Mr.
and Mrs. Doolittle—true saints of God. Mrs. Doolittle had been bedridden for nigh twenty years.
Her husband was an incurable cripple who had
to propel himself to and from his business in a
wheel chair. Despite their afflictions, they lived
happy Christian lives, bringing inspiration and
comfort to all who knew them. One day while
we were visiting with the Doolittles, my husband
commented on their bright hopefulness and
asked them for the secret of it. Mrs. Doolittle's
reply was simple: "His eye is on the sparrow, and I
know He watches me." The beauty of this simple
expression of boundless faith gripped the hearts
and fired the imagination of Dr. Martin and me.
The hymn "His Eye Is on the Sparrow" was the
outcome of that experience.

As the Doolittles show us, it's this *enchanted sense of
significance* that makes meaning *durable* and *sturdy* in the
face of failure, pain, and setback. But without God, without the enchantment of mattering, we lose this resiliency.
All we have in this skeptical age is vulnerability, anxiety,
and fragility. All we have is the Ache.

We've got one more stop on our tour.

RICHARD BECK

During the enchanted age, five hundred years ago, the self was vulnerable to invasion from outside forces. Our ancestors worried about spells and curses. The most extreme example of this invasion—demon possession—was a real threat. The philosopher Charles Taylor has described this enchanted experience of the self as "porous," a self with holes and gaps in the walls making it vulnerable to attacks from the outside world. Taylor contrasts this "porous" self with our modern, disenchanted self, a self that is now "buffered," closed and walled off from the supernatural and demonic threats in the world.

Closed off as it is from the external world, our modern, buffered self has become increasingly focused and preoccupied with what's happening on the *inside*. We've become increasingly *self*-absorbed, obsessed with our interior life. No longer fearing demons invading and possessing us, we now speak about battling our "inner demons," all our psychological baggage, our self-defeating habits, compulsions, addictions, and emotional issues. Where the *enchanted self* once looked outward, the *disenchanted self* now looks inward. Our daily battles are no longer *spiritual* struggles with dark forces in the world but *therapeutic* struggles for self-control and healing.

The dawn of this inward-looking self changed how we pursue and secure purpose and meaning. The enchanted self didn't just look *outward* to monitor supernatural threats; it also looked *upward* for supernatural direction

58

and guidance. We navigated life in the enchanted age by looking toward God as our guiding North Star. Meaning and purpose were secured when we aligned ourselves with the will of God.

But the modern self doesn't look outward and upward. The modern self turns *inward*. We find our purpose by *going deep* to discover our "true selves" and then staying true to that self. And there's a whole cottage industry out there that can help us locate this true, authentic self. We can take tests, read books, attend seminars, get a life coach, or go to therapy. But no matter how we find it, once we locate our true self, we set it as our North Star. We draft a life mission statement, identify our strengths, pick our "word for the year," and then set our course. We obtain meaning and purpose by living *authentically*, by staying true to ourselves.

But therein lies a problem.

I don't know if you've noticed, but it can be pretty hard to disentangle your inner demons from your true self. These can actually be the same thing. This is perhaps the greatest lesson Sigmund Freud taught the modern world: that we are masters of self-deception. Our "true" desires and motivations are not very easy to spot or recognize. Mainly because there's some ugly stuff lurking down there in the shadowy basement of the self. So we tend to build our self-image out of the lies we tell ourselves. Our identities are webs spun with avoidance and denial. Which makes the quest for "authenticity"—being true to yourself—a bit of a fool's errand. Our self-deception handicaps our ability to live happily and healthily. We can't make decisions that are good for us if we're laboring under a false image of ourselves. How often have you looked in the mirror and asked, "What the hell is wrong with you? Why can't you get your act together?" The experience of the modern self is one of confusion and befuddlement.

And even if you were able to locate your "true self," it doesn't sit still for very long. As a college professor, I watch my students courageously pursuing the modern ethic of authenticity. No one prizes authenticity like millennials and Gen Zers. But I also watch how many times my students change their majors, swinging wildly from one vocational dream to another. Millennials and Gen Zers are desperately trying to chart their course in life by following the North Star of their "true self." The trouble is, that star keeps moving around. As their "true self" bounces around, their lives become less authentic and more schizophrenic. This changing self isn't unique to young adults. Ever hear of a thing called a midlife crisis? The self isn't a rock, a stable feature in our psyche that never changes. The self is volatile, fickle, and jumpy. So if your "true self" is a constantly moving target, how are you ever going to settle down into your authentic life?

The thing to see here is that the modern, disenchanted self is a *neurotic* self, a self that is both self-absorbed and deeply unstable and unsettled. When the modern world turned inward for meaning, direction, and purpose—when we turned away from God to raise the banner of authenticity—we made a devil's bargain. In declaring our independence from God, we became anxious and neurotic. Just look around—the skeptical, disenchanted world is deeply and profoundly unwell.

Welcome to the Ache.

Our tour is over, and the train is now returning to the station.

What have we seen on our tour of the Ache? This: We are deeply dissatisfied with disenchantment. Disenchantment is making us sick, and we recoil in horror at the world it has given us, a world stripped of its holy, sacred character. We need to hallow. We need to pray. We need creation to be a church—sacred, holy, and set apart. We need to matter in the face of failure and heartbreak. And we need a North Star more constant than ourselves.

Again, the Ache doesn't prove the existence of God. But when we trace the contours of our pain, we cultivate *a sense of dissatisfaction with our skeptical age*, even a sense of horror and disgust. This profound dissatisfaction with the bill of goods being sold to us by the modern world is our first step back toward enchantment. The Ache is, quite simply, our thirst for enchantment and our longing for God.

So let your finger trace the edges of our pain and insecurity. Connect all the dots. Then step back and take a look at the figure you have drawn. Ponder the shape of the Ache, because you're looking at the chalk outline of God.

3

WHY GOOD PEOPLE
NEED GOD

He was a Christian ministry major at my university and having a faith crisis. Or at least having some serious questions about his vocational calling to serve as a pastor in a church. The cause of the crisis, the source of his doubting, was simple: some of his dearest friends were atheists and agnostics, and they were among the most loving people he knew. "In fact," he shared with me, "my atheist friends are more loving than most of the Christians I know." And that moral contrast—loving atheists versus unkind Christians—was calling his faith and career into question. If people can be good without God, if atheists can be more loving than followers of Jesus, then what's the point of Christianity and the church?

The faith crisis of the ministry major is very common. As I shared in chapter 1, the greatest threat to the church in the modern world is the moralization and politicization of faith. The goal of life is to be a good person. Loving, kind, and tolerant. And if you can be loving, kind, and tolerant without God, then God is deemed irrelevant and superfluous. Worse, if there's a chance God will make you hateful and bigoted, why risk it? Best to keep clear of the whole religious train wreck to focus simply on being kind. Seems like a safe and sane course of action.

I have a lot of sympathy for that ministry major. Given all the church scandals, from megachurch pastors involved in sexual harassment to Catholic priests involved in child abuse, Christianity is a damaged brand, and a lot of us want to distance ourselves from this toxic association. We are embarrassed by the church. Perhaps distancing ourselves from Christianity is the most Christian thing we can do right now. That has been the biggest pushback I've received since the publication of this book. Is the crisis of faith in the modern world due to disenchantment or to the moral failures of the church? Because we're sick and tired of all the church scandals, and disgusted by people waving Jesus flags as they smash in the windows of the United States Capitol.

Given the obvious failures of the church, I am hesitant to share why I think good people might need God. Maybe it would be best to leave the good people alone. Especially given the sorry state of Christianity. The church should clean up its own act before it starts pointing fingers. As it says in First Peter 4:17, let the judgment of God begin first with the household of God. Let's remove the beam out of our own eye before picking at a speck in the eye of an atheist. As Paul says in First Corinthians 5:12, what business is it of ours to judge the world? Our job, says Paul, is to judge those on the *inside* of the church. That is very wise advice. Let us, as Christians, police our own tribe. That would be time and energy well spent.

And yet, I do think good people need God. Let me share why.

Yesterday I was surrounded by calls to kindness. It was unavoidable. Driving around the city, I saw it on car windows and bumper stickers. I saw it on laptops at the coffee shop. I saw it on social media memes. "Be Kind." "Be a Kind Human Being." "Practice Random Acts of Kindness."

In case you missed it, kindness is the new cool. And I'm happy about this. Jesus is winning.

Atheism might be on the rise, and fewer people might be going to church, but the modern world is deeply Christian. Atheists are deeply Christian. Pagans are deeply Christian. Social justice warriors are deeply Christian. Haters of Christianity are deeply Christian. You can see it right there in the complaint that atheists are often more loving than Christians. Love is the measure of our moral lives. For everyone. Love is the scale upon which we are being weighed in the balance, Christian and non-Christian alike. Just ask John Lennon: "All you need is love!" Love is the ethic of our modern world.

Like it or not, it was the Judeo-Christian tradition that made "Love Wins" and "Be Kind" the mantras of the Western world. The social justice movement started with Moses saying to Pharaoh, "Let my people go!" and the Hebrew prophets shouting, "Let justice flow down like a river!" Where the Greco-Roman world valorized power, dominance, and military victory, Jesus embodied mercy and compassion and set the world ablaze in a moral firestorm that is still fiercely burning. Every "Be Kind" sticker on cars or laptops originated with St. Paul and First Corinthians 13, "Love is patient, love is kind." Before Christianity, kindness was failure, shame, and weakness. Today, kindness is cool. Like I said, Jesus is winning.

Maybe good people don't need God to be good, but God gives us our definition of *good*. And it goes deeper than that. The problem with kindness being cool is that kindness could become a fashion accessory. A lifestyle choice. But most of the truly kind people I know don't see it that way. Kindness, for them, is a sacred duty and obligation: We ought to be kind even when we don't want to be kind. We can't opt out. I think most of us share this sensibility, or aspire to it. Everyone ought to be kind. No exceptions. Kindness isn't a fashion choice. I'm not morally offended if you wear blue to work. But I am offended if you're unkind at work. You should do better. We can disagree about fashion, but we can't disagree about how to treat each other.

My point here is that, beyond our definition of goodness, we've also inherited from the Judeo-Christian tradition the sense that goodness is more than an opinion or personal preference, something you can opt out of on a whim. In our secular world we don't know where this feeling comes from, that everyone ought to be kind, but we feel it nonetheless. We have these Christian emotions without the Christian beliefs. We can't defend these feelings any longer, but we feel them deeply in our bones. Everyone ought to be kind, and we're upset when people are not. That's why we put "Be Kind" stickers on our laptops and cars.

But truth be told, we're not very kind people. Even the kindest people have their limits. Whenever I hear someone say, "I know atheists who are kinder than Christians," they don't mean kinder to *everyone*. They don't mean *unconditionally* kind. What they mean is kinder *to the right kind of people*. Our kindness is narrow, conditional, and exclusive.

Just take a look at how a conditional kindness characterizes our political lives. Over the last few election cycles, social scientists have been tracking the disturbing rise of what is called "affective polarization" within the American electorate. Different from issue polarization, such as how we feel about policy proposals, affective polarization concerns the feelings we have about the *people* on the other side of the political aisle—the feelings Democrats have about Republicans and Republicans about Democrats. A 2019 study on affective polarization in the *Annual Review of Political Science* summarized the situation: "Ordinary Americans increasingly dislike and distrust those from the other party. Democrats and Republicans both say that the other party's members are hypocritical, selfish, and closed-minded, and they are unwilling to socialize across party lines."

We've witnessed affective polarization on Facebook and at Thanksgiving dinners, tempers flaring when friends and family members express dismaying political opinions. Affective polarization explains why our political conversations have become so difficult, tense, and unproductive: we're demonizing our conversation partners. The possibility of compromise evaporates because seeking common ground is viewed as evidence of moral failure, caving in to the forces of evil. No ground can be ceded in this struggle. Kindness to enemies is betrayal.

How many of us practice kindness, love, and charity to political opponents? Few. Those who do practice unconditional kindness do so because they consider it a sacred duty and obligation, a transcendent value that cannot be broken, no matter how you vote. Enchantment

is what keeps kindness from being thrown into the trash
can every election cycle. Without this enchantment, kindness becomes narrow and exclusive, a grace extended to
the lucky, like-minded few.

There's also the issue regarding the emotional sustainability of kindness and compassion in the face of troubling
news reports and our incessant doom-scrolling through
social media. Although the secular world inherited the
"Love Wins" ethic of the Judeo-Christian tradition, we
jettisoned the enchanted beliefs that once catalyzed and
sustained the associated emotions. Our emotions once
had a solid foundation and supportive walls. But stripped
of this sacred support, love and compassion have been
reduced to feelings, an inner glow I have to conjure up
through sheer force of will, over and over again, day
after day, in the face of steady news of tragedy, devastation, and injustice. Keeping our hearts compassionately
engaged becomes exhausting, like blowing up a balloon
when we're all out of breath.

Psychologists call this experience empathy or compassion fatigue. I expect you've experienced this. We've
inherited from Christianity the emotional expectation
that we, as good people, should care about all the world's
suffering. We are to love everyone, care about every
victim, ache over every harm, and rage against every

69

injustice. Good people care about all the things, all the time. Indifference isn't a moral option. But step back for a moment and ponder the emotional sustainability of this expectation. Is your heart able to carry the pain of the entire world? Day in and day out, without succumbing to hopelessness and despair?

Without enchantment, universal compassion is an unsustainable prospect. We see evidence of this everywhere. Post-Christian people cannot handle their social media feeds without massive amounts of compassion fatigue dragging them into depression or panic attacks. People are burning out and falling apart.

Christian hope once sustained our compassion with the conviction that any small act of love makes a lasting, eternal difference. Once upon a time, we believed what Julian of Norwich believed, that "all shall be well, and all manner of thing shall be well." Faith sustained our troubled, exhausted hearts. This enchanted view of history also fueled the activism of Dr. Martin Luther King Jr., who declared that "the arc of the moral universe is long, but it bends toward justice." Hope sustains our faithful, daily engagement with the pain of the world, and pushes back against the feeling that nothing we do will ever make a difference.

I have more to say about hope in chapter 7, but for now let me simply state the obvious: Good people in the modern world are facing an unsustainable emotional predicament. As the children of Christianity, we believe we should be loving and compassionate. But as post-Christian moderns who have rejected the enchantment that called us to love, we find the demands of compassion exhausting. Without hope, our hearts grow tired and our mental health deteriorates with each troubling news cycle. Yes, there are many good people in the world, but without God, the pain of the world becomes a burden too heavy for us to bear.

In the psychological care of war veterans, there's a phenomenon called "moral injury." War is horrible and traumatic, and soldiers are often placed in situations where they must act in ways, or witness acts, that damage their conscience. This scarring of conscience is called moral injury. Among solders returning from combat, moral injury is associated with PTSD, depression, suicide, and addiction.

Most of us are spared moral injury to the scale produced by the horrors of war, but we all experience moral injury. Even good people. We've all behaved in ways that have damaged our conscience. Everyone carries soul wounds.

Moral injury is a reason good people need God. I'm reminded of the commencement address delivered by the novelist George Saunders at Syracuse University. Saunders tells the story of a girl named Ellen who was in the seventh grade with him. Socially awkward, Ellen was teased and shunned. Forty-two years later, Saunders was still haunted by those memories, wishing he had been a better friend to Ellen. At the climax of his graduation speech, Saunders stated it plainly: "What I regret most about my life are failures of kindness." So do I. I have these same regrets. I bet you do as well. To say nothing of those times when we've actually hurt and harmed other people. Our lives are filled with moral injury. Sins of commission and sins of omission. Things we have done and things we have failed to do. And there's a sad paradox here as well: the better a person you are, the more your conscience haunts you.

Sure, there are good people in the world. And maybe they don't need to be better than they already are. But the shadow cast by our goodness is the haunted conscience. Good people might not need God in order to be good, but they do need God for grace.

There's a petition from the Liturgy of the Hours that always interrupts me. It's a petition prayed on Fridays, reflecting upon the penitential psalms. The petition pleads, "Heal our wounded conscience." I need that prayer every Friday because I can't make it seven days without sustaining some sort of moral injury. I'll confess, I've been trying to be a good person for over fifty years and I don't think I've made a ton of progress. Week after week the prayer I most crave and need is "Heal my wounded conscience."

Of course, we shouldn't use grace to escape our hard responsibilities in making things right. If it is within our power, we must make amends. But as all the guilty know, you can do everything possible to make things right and still be haunted by shame and guilt. You can't get clean. You are unable lay the burden down. Moral injuries are not so easily healed.

What makes the way of Jesus so potent and powerful for good but disenchanted people is its paradoxical mixture of radical goodness and radical grace. It's really quite remarkable. Christianity calls you to the impossible heights of love, that unconditional call to kindness, yet recognizes in the very same breath your moral frailty and vulnerability. Even good people, and perhaps good people most of all, need healing for their wounded conscience.

I recently had a mystical experience. It wasn't long, just a flash. I was walking and stubbed my toe, causing me to stumble forward. Instinctively, I reached out my hand to touch the wall and prevent my fall. In that moment, I heard an internal voice (or my own mind—I couldn't tell which) say, "This is prayer."

In the months since, I've kept revisiting that experience. I return, over and over, to the central insight: *When we are falling, we reach out to make contact with something sturdier than ourselves.*

RICHARD BECK

Life is hard. As I described in chapter 2, we're lost and hurting. So while good people may be good, that doesn't mean we're happy, joyful, and thriving. We're dealing with stress, anxiety, and sadness. We're holding broken dreams and disappointments. We're lonely. We're stuck in unfulfilling jobs. We're falling. And when we're falling, we need to reach out and make contact with something sturdier than ourselves. We pray that prayer of "Help!"

When I look at my college students, two things immediately jump out at me. First, my students care about oppression. They are *woke*. They are social justice warriors. They are activists. My students live in a highly charged moral universe. Some have described the social justice movement as a "new Puritanism," even a new religion that is replacing Christianity in our culture.

The second thing that jumps out, as I described in chapter 2, is that my students are anxious and depressed. Our youth are experiencing a crisis of meaning that is having a pervasive and adverse impact on their mental health.

These two things—a highly charged, puritanical moralism and emotional distress—are intimately linked.

To start, the trends are linked historically. As I mentioned, the social justice movement preserved the core of the Judeo-Christian ethic—"Love Wins"—while rejecting its metaphysical, narrative, sacramental, and communal infrastructure. Trouble was, it was this metaphysical, narrative, sacramental, and communal infrastructure that once provided us with deep and rich meaning-making resources and pathways. An intense moralism has been carried over from the past, but has been stripped of the enchantments that provided us with hope, joy, peace, and shared purpose.

Beyond history, the trends are also linked psychologically. Stringent moral performance has never made anyone happy, light, free, and joyous. Puritanism, old or new, is a grim affair. It isn't news to anyone that supercharged activist circles are angsty, angry, and anxious. Activists are winning the goodness game, as all Pharisees will, but they are emotionally unwell. Puritanism isn't healthy or sustainable.

Does that mean my social justice warrior students should give up the fight? That we should stop being woke and go back to sleep? Of course not. Keep awake and keep fighting! But what does have to happen is that the puritanical moralism of social justice activism has to be re-embedded into the metaphysical, narrative, sacramental, and communal matrix that birthed and sustained that moral vision. The enchantments of this larger religious matrix provide resources for rest, grace, mercy, peace, fellowship, joy, wonder, beauty, and meaning. When moral performance, even stringent moral performance, is embedded within this matrix, it becomes psychologically and relationally sustainable. Meaning in life is more than strict moral performance. Good people are good, but they are also lost and hurting. Good people need enchantment because they need more than goodness; they need healing for the Ache.

In 2016, Michelle Alexander, author of the book *The New Jim Crow*, in which she recounts the injustices of mass incarceration upon Black America, resigned from her position as a law professor at Ohio State to join Union Theological Seminary. In sharing her reasons for stepping away from the law to teach in a seminary, Alexander shared this on Facebook:

> Who am I to teach or study at a seminary? I was not raised in a church. And I have generally found more questions than answers in my own religious or spiritual pursuits. But I also know there is something much greater at stake in justice work than we often acknowledge. Solving the crises we face isn't simply a matter of having the right facts, graphs, policy analyses, or funding. And I no longer believe we can "win" justice simply by filing lawsuits, flexing our political muscles or boosting voter turnout. Yes, we absolutely must do that work, but none of it—not even working for some form of political revolution— will ever be enough on its own. Without a moral

or spiritual awakening, we will remain forever trapped in political games fueled by fear, greed and the hunger for power. . . .

This is not simply a legal problem, or a political problem, or a policy problem. At its core, America's journey from slavery to Jim Crow to mass incarceration raises profound moral and spiritual questions about who we are, individually and collectively, who we aim to become, and what we are willing to do now.

I have found that these questions are generally not asked or answered in law schools or policy roundtables. So I am going to a place that takes very seriously the moral, ethical and spiritual dimensions of justice work.

Social justice warriors like my students need God because life is morally complicated. As Alexander points out, the moral worldview of the social justice movement without God is too narrow, impoverished, and simplistic to deal with the moral complexity of the world. Social justice needs enchantment if it is to take "very seriously the moral, ethical, and spiritual dimension of justice work." Good people need God because, if we want to solve the problems facing us, we need "a moral and spiritual awakening." We need enchantment.

As the saying goes, when all you have is a hammer, everything starts to look like a nail. Justice is just one tool in our moral toolbox. A critical, essential tool. But one tool can't do all the moral work life demands of us. Justice is a hammer, and when you're looking at a nail— say, oppression—the hammer is the tool to pick up. But the moral drama of our lives isn't just about oppression. We're dealing with all sorts of things, from forgiveness to mercy to shame to guilt to joy to truth to peace to reconciliation. And hitting mercy with a hammer just isn't a good idea. You'll break it.

Consider an obvious example: how the social justice movement struggles with the issue of forgiveness. With the pervasiveness of what has been called "cancel culture," can the canceled ever be forgiven? What about problematic allies? What if someone's moral performance for the cause is less than perfect? The social justice movement struggles here with the issues of mercy, grace, forgiveness, and reconciliation. The reason for this is that justice is a hammer, and while a hammer is an excellent tool for nails, it is not so great with other moral tasks. Forgiveness is a different problem than injustice. You need different tools. The moral drama of life isn't putting up a swing set in the backyard, easily tackled with the single tool enclosed in the box; it's building an entire house. Moral life is cement work, brick laying, carpentry, plumbing, electrical, roofing, painting, and so on. You need more than a hammer.

Good people need God, as Michelle Alexander pointed out, so that we can grow up and into a richer, more complex moral universe, a deeper moral vocabulary that matches the complexities of our lives. Only religion provides us with such a deep, rich, various, and multifaceted moral toolbox.

A final thing I'd like to say about good people needing God is that sometimes you're the one needing to be loved. That's what makes a church different from a protest or working for a nonprofit. Churches exist to care about you. I know the church is a damaged brand. Yes, I've listened to the *Rise and Fall of Mars Hill* podcast, recounting the tragic fall of the megachurch pastor Mark Driscoll. I understand the wariness surrounding churches. But it would do your heart good to find a healthy church in your town. A place where people know you and care about you. Going to church is less about moral self-improvement than about giving and receiving love, especially during those times when you're the one needing to be carried. Spiritually, emotionally, relationally, fiscally, materially, physically, and medically. Find a caring church. You'll be happy you did.

I will not blame anyone for being hesitant about God or church. And with everyone wanting to be kind, Jesus is winning anyway. But when kindness gets hard, you need the enchantment of sacred duties and obligations to make it more than a cool bumper sticker. Love is the greatest virtue, but it requires the enchantments of faith and hope to make it emotionally sustainable in the face of troubling news reports. We also need grace when we experience moral injury, those greatest regrets in life. Life is hard, and we need healing for the Ache. Looking out at the world, the social problems facing us are huge and we're going to need more than a hammer. A spiritual revolution is needed. And lastly, we need a place to go where people love and care for us. Such a place exists, right where you live. Give it a chance.

PART 2

ENCHANTED FAITH

4

ECCENTRIC
EXPERIENCES

In 1967, Johnny Cash crawled into Nickajack Cave planning to kill himself. The year had been the darkest of Cash's life. His life had spiraled out of control because of his drug addiction, promoters were canceling his shows because of his erratic behavior, and his wife, Vivian, had filed for divorce.

Wracked by grief and guilt, Cash drove to the cave with a plan to bring an end to it all. For sure, it wasn't a very rational or lethal plan. Cash was probably high when he concocted it. He was going to crawl deep into the cave to get lost in the maze of its tunnels, so lost he'd never be able to find his way back out again. Cash entered and climbed through the cave system until the batteries of his flashlight died. Left in absolute darkness, Cash lay down in the inky blackness and waited to die.

And there, in the midst of his pain, God spoke to Johnny Cash. Cash heard a voice whisper to him, "I am still here." Though Cash had wandered far from God, he realized there in the darkness that God had never abandoned him.

The voice Cash heard in the darkness of Nickajack Cave proved to be a turning point in his life. After hearing God's voice, Cash crawled out of the cave and back into the light.

Mystical encounters with God, what psychologists call "religious experiences," come in many shapes and sizes. Sometimes God shows up in an audible voice, like when Johnny Cash heard God whisper to him "I am still here" in the darkness of Nickajack Cave. Others have seen visions. There have been encounters with angels. I have friends who have witnessed miracles.

For others, God comes less in miracles and visions than in intimations, in sharpened perceptions and deepened emotions. I've never heard the voice of God like Johnny Cash did. I experience God in profound feelings of peace, joy, and love and even in sad feelings when my heart breaks for the pain of the world, emotions that overwhelm me to the point of tears. It's very hard to put these experiences into words. That's one of the defining characteristics of these moments—how words fail us in capturing them. But I'd like us to try. Doing so will help us pay better attention to the strange sights all around us.

In 1901 and 1902, the famous philosopher and psychologist William James delivered the Gifford Lectures in Scotland. The lectures were eventually published in a book entitled *The Varieties of Religious Experience*, a book that would go on to have an enormous influence on the fields of psychology and religion. *The Varieties* is still widely read today, and I assign it to my students. In my world, when you refer to "King James," you're not talking about a Bible translation or LeBron. You're talking about William James and *The Varieties of Religious Experience*.

In *The Varieties*, James attempts something very ambitious: a description of religious experience. Fundamentally, and this is why James will be helpful to us, a religious experience is a *perception*. As James observes, a religious experience is "a sense of reality, a feeling of objective presence, a perception of what we might call 'something there,' more deep and more general" than what our regular senses reveal to us. Sometimes this is an experience of divine presence, like what Johnny Cash experienced in Nickajack Cave. Sometimes the experience is simply the insight that reality is more—deeper, wider, more connected than we'd imagined. This description is helpful and encouraging because we too quickly assume that bumping into God means something big and miraculous, like seeing visions of angels. But if religious experiences are *perceptions of More*—encountering a reality more real, more enchanted, more related, more alive, more loving, more sacred, more holy—then I expect a lot of us have had experiences like these throughout our lives. We've felt, sensed, intuited, or seen—and again, words are going to fail me here—that the world is richer and more wondrous than what we typically perceive in day-to-day life. These perceptions, subtle or overwhelming, the thundering voice of God or the still, small voice, come to us as we stand under a starlit sky or witness the birth of a child. They come to us as we stand on a street corner like Thomas Merton and feel overwhelmed with love for total strangers. In my life, these moments come from out of nowhere, in pretty random locations, my heart suddenly flooded with a beautiful longing. Our lives are filled with these sensations, perceptions, emotions, and intuitions. Religious experiences are like Peter Parker's "spider sense," a sacred tingling we feel when God has just shown up. When we widen our view and don't reduce God to visions, voices, and angelic visitations, we discover that we bump into God all the time. Slowly, if we practice paying attention, we come to see the dancing gorilla right in front of us.

The most famous lecture in *The Varieties of Religious Experience* is James's chapter on mysticism. If people only read one chapter of *The Varieties of Religious Experience*, this is the chapter they read. It's fascinating because of how James went about his investigations. James approached mystical experiences like a butterfly or stamp collector. James searched high and low for examples of mystical experiences, asking regular people to share their experiences with him but also poring over the memoirs and biographies of saints and famous religious figures. As a collector, James didn't care much about the source of the experience. He collected experiences from across the world religions, from Christianity to Hinduism. He also collected experiences that weren't particularly religious in nature. His goal in gathering such a large and diverse collection of mystical experiences was to look for common features, shared characteristics that showed up over and over. All told, James felt that four ingredients make up an encounter with the sacred and holy.

The first characteristic of an encounter with God is one I've already mentioned: ineffability. Religious experiences are hard to put into words. There's something about encountering God that defies verbal description. Recall what Thomas Merton said on the corner of Fourth and Walnut: "If only everybody could realize this! But it cannot be explained." Words fail.

The ineffable nature of these encounters and perceptions explains why art and music are so often the most effective language of faith. The re-enchantment of faith will lean more heavily on beauty and aesthetics than upon logical arguments. As Dostoevsky once said, "Beauty will save the world." Music, art, poetry, and architecture, along with the wonders of the natural world, are much better equipped to capture and communicate the ineffable nature of spiritual insights and truths. Our faith will struggle when it becomes excessively verbal and rational. In my experience, Christians who struggle with disenchantment lean too heavily on words. Too many books and podcasts. Too much talking. Disenchantment is often a sign that you've lost touch with the aesthetic, ineffable aspects of faith. If you're struggling with disenchantment, odds are you're *thinking* rather than paying *attention*.

The mystical tradition of Christianity has always known that the best way to encounter God is to stop talking and start looking. There's a famous story about St. Thomas Aquinas, perhaps the greatest theologian of all time. Thomas had spent most of this life writing and thinking about God. Toward the end of his life, he was working on his greatest work, the *Summa Theologia*, considered by many to be the most significant theological book ever written. But Thomas never finished it. On December 6, 1273, while celebrating the Mass, Thomas had a mystical experience that caused him to stop writing the *Summa*. When his assistant urged him to continue and finish the book, Thomas answered, "I cannot, because all that I have written seems like straw to me."

Whatever Thomas saw during Mass that day, it pushed his words, some of the most influential words about God ever written, past the breaking point. When it comes to God, words get left behind. Even for St. Thomas.

Blaise Pascal (1623–62) was a famous mathematician, scientist, and inventor. He was also a mystic, which makes him a wonderful example of how a person devoted to analysis, logic, and reason can still bump into God from time to time.

The most significant mystical experience of Pascal's life occurred on November 23, 1654. The experience lasted two hours, beginning at 10:30 p.m. and ending at 12:30 a.m. We know these details because, after Pascal's death, it was discovered that he had sewn a handwritten account of the experience inside his jacket to keep it close to his heart. This is what Pascal experienced, in his own words:

The year of grace 1654,

Monday, 23 November, feast of St. Clement, pope and martyr, and others in the martyrology.
Vigil of St. Chrysogonus, martyr, and others.
From about half past ten at night until about half past midnight,

FIRE.

GOD of Abraham, GOD of Isaac, GOD of Jacob
not of the philosophers and of the learned.
Certitude. Certitude. Feeling. Joy. Peace.
GOD of Jesus Christ.
My God and your God.
Your GOD will be my God.
Forgetfulness of the world and of everything, except GOD.
He is only found by the ways taught in the Gospel.
Grandeur of the human soul.
Righteous Father, the world has not known you, but I have
    known you.
Joy, joy, joy, tears of joy.
I have departed from him:
They have forsaken me, the fount of living water.
My God, will you leave me?
Let me not be separated from him forever.
This is eternal life, that they know you, the one true God,
    and the one that you sent,
Jesus Christ.
Jesus Christ.
Jesus Christ.
I left him; I fled him, renounced, crucified.
Let me never be separated from him.
He is only kept securely by the ways taught in the Gospel:
Renunciation, total and sweet.
Complete submission to Jesus Christ and to my director.

Eternally in joy for a day's exercise on the earth.
May I not forget your words. Amen.

Pascal's mystical experience—his encounter with a "FIRE" that filled him with joy—illustrates the second feature of religious experiences. Mystical experiences are transitory and short lived. Pascal's experience of fire lasted two hours, then it was over. Personally, I've never had an experience with God that lasted that long. I think for many of us, religious experiences are more like lightning strikes—sharp, quick flashes of perception and awareness that briefly illuminate our lives. Sometimes the experience is soft and gentle, like a lightning bug on a summer evening, glowing for an instant and then fading back to darkness.

Given their transitory nature, mystical experiences have to be held, recalled, and preserved. The sacred truths revealed to us in these moments need to be carried forward. Otherwise, they fade and are forgotten. This is why Pascal stitched an account of his mystical experience inside his coat. He needed reminding.

We all need reminding. Because I want us to be realistic about enchantment. We need to be open to the reality of encountering God everywhere and in every place, but we can't assume life will crackle with magic 24-7. And we won't have burning bush moments in every moment of prayer or worship. The truth is, there will be seasons, perhaps long ones, where God will go quiet. We can experience what St. John of the Cross called a "dark night of the soul," where our spiritual lives are characterized by a sharp sense of God's absence. During these seasons, enchantment becomes *a discipline of memory.* Just like Mary did in the gospels, we treasure moments in our hearts. We write them down and stitch them to the insides of our coats. During the dark night of the soul, enchantment is less about forcing God to appear than fidelity to the moments that have been graced to us. For even the absence of God is an enchantment. There's a difference between an empty hole and an empty stomach. An empty hole points to a void. An empty stomach knows it is meant for something. The pain of the dark night isn't an empty hole. Our longing is a *hunger,* a sign that we are meant for God and that we are not complete without God. We yearn for the Grace we know exists because of what we have stitched to the inside of our coats. We remember.

The fact that we can't force or control these moments highlights the third feature of mystical experiences. William James called it "passivity." What James means by passivity is that we can't make the moment happen; the moment happens to us. Something from outside of ourselves grabs or interrupts us. Mystical experiences are not *manufactured;* they are *received.*

As the theologian David Kelsey has pointed out, our life with God is "eccentric." Enchantment comes to us from the *outside*. Mystical experiences are gifts.

Enchantment is eccentric as it's an outward-facing posture of expectancy and receptivity. This posture of receptivity is *the posture of grace*, receiving our lives as gifts. The Greek word in the Bible for *grace* is also the word for *gift*. And gifts are eccentric in that they are received and come to us from the outside. We adopt this *posture of gift* whenever we offer up prayers of Thanks, Help, and Wow. These prayers turn our attention outward in expressions of gratitude, dependency, and wonder.

I'm going to stop here for now, since this *outward turn*, adopting an eccentric posture toward life, is going to be a huge part of our conversation going forward. Lots more to share.

The fourth and last mark of mystical experiences is that these moments possess what William James calls a "noetic quality." The word *noetic* comes from the Greek word *noeó*, meaning "to perceive, see, or understand." This is the word Jesus uses a lot in the gospels when his disciples cannot see a point he is trying to make. "Do you not *see?*" Jesus repeatedly asks his disciples.

Mystical experiences are not emotional highs; they are *revelations*. As William James describes it, mystical experiences are felt to be "states of knowledge . . . insight into depths of truths unplumbed" by our minds and intelligence. Mystical experiences are "illuminations, revelations, full of significance and importance." These illuminations and revelations do trigger strong emotions, but fundamentally they are about perceiving or seeing something concerning the nature of reality. Pascal's experience filled him with "joy, joy, joy," but those feelings were in response to an encounter with the "GOD of Abraham, GOD of Isaac, GOD of Jacob." Pascal's joy flowed out of a sense of insight and knowledge, a "certitude." Think again about Thomas Merton's experience on Fourth and Walnut. He also experienced an emotional high, an experience of "immense joy." But that joy was triggered by the noetic quality of the experience. As Merton wrote, "Now I realize what we all are. . . . [We] are all walking around shining like the sun." Just like Pascal, first came the *realization*, the *perception*, the *seeing*. Then came the joy.

The biblical word for the noetic quality of mystical experiences is *apocalypse*. Contrary to what many people think, the word *apocalypse* doesn't mean "world-ending cataclysm." In the Bible, the word *apocalypse* simply means "unveiling," as in "to uncover or reveal something that had been hidden." Mystical experiences are apocalypses, revelations, and unveilings, windows into a deeper reality.

An apocalyptic understanding of mystical experiences helps us enchant our faith in this skeptical age because we have very narrow expectations about what bumping into God might feel or look like. We think it's always supposed to be something stunning and spectacular, hearing the audible voice of God like Johnny Cash in Nickajack Cave. But if a mystical experience is an *apocalypse*, we're having these experiences all the time.

The diversity of these apocalyptic moments is revealed if you take a tour through the mystical experiences found in the Bible. Let's consider three important examples: assurance, mission, and conviction.

Sometimes the apocalypse is a revelation about your identity, an assurance of God's love. Consider Jesus's experience at his baptism. When Jesus comes up out of the water, he hears his Father declare, "You are my Beloved, in whom I delight." Jesus begins his ministry with this unveiling, moving into the world with an assurance of his Father's approval and love. Many of us have had experiences just like Jesus's, a strongly felt sense of God's love and approval. A famous example of this comes from the life of John Wesley, the founder of Methodism. On May 24, 1738, Wesley heard a reading from Martin Luther concerning the gospel of grace. Listening to that message, Wesley felt his heart "strangely warmed." That flood of emotion was an apocalypse, a revelation of God's love. As Wesley proclaimed about that moment, "Assurance was given me." I bet you've had experiences just like this, your heart strangely warmed by the apocalypse of grace. An intense experience of God's love is poured out

upon us. Perhaps you felt this in your conversion experience, but these moments show up throughout our lives.
In listening to a song, reading a poem, hearing a sermon,
reading a book, walking in nature, or simply savoring a
moment, we find our hearts strangely warmed by grace
and love: "You are my beloved child, in whom I delight."

Beyond an assurance of grace, sometimes bumping
into God places a calling on lives, gives us a mission.
Moses's encounter with the Lord at the burning bush is a
great example. Moses is sent to Pharaoh with the demand,
"Let my people go!" Think also of young Samuel hearing the voice of God in the night (1 Samuel 3) or Isaiah's
vision of God in the temple (Isaiah 6). In each case, both
Samuel and Isaiah make themselves available to God's
calling. As Isaiah says, "Here am I; send me!" I bet you've
also had experiences like this, moments where God
placed a call on your heart to which you felt compelled
to respond. John Wesley's experience of having his heart
"strangely warmed" didn't just fill him with an assurance
of grace; it filled him with evangelistic passion, causing
him to become one of the most influential evangelists of
all time. In a similar way, on September 10, 1946, Mother
(now Saint) Teresa was riding on a train from Calcutta
to a retreat in the Himalayan foothills. On the train ride,
Jesus spoke to Teresa, telling her to abandon her vocation
as a teacher to work in the slums of Calcutta to care for
the city's poorest and sickest people. In my life, my work
in a prison flowed from a similar conviction, a spiritual

call to seek and find God among the incarcerated. Stories like these fill my church, and I bet your church as well. My friends have been called by God to foster or adopt children, to start nonprofits, to get sober, to volunteer for community service, to be better neighbors, to join a protest, or redevote themselves to their marriages, parenting, or friendships. We get that "spider sense" tingling, nudging us to invite someone to coffee, call a friend, or offer some small encouragement to a coworker. God isn't silent or absent. God is calling you all the time. We just have to listen and make ourselves available: "Here I am. Send me."

Lastly, and in a related way, these revelations can be experienced as moral convictions, moments that expose how our love needs to expand, to embrace those whom we've ignored or excluded. Think of Peter's vision of unclean animals in Acts 10. Peter falls into a trance on a rooftop and sees a sheet full of unclean animals being lowered from heaven. A voice says to Peter, "Get up, Peter; kill and eat." Peter refuses, objecting that the animals are unclean, not kosher to eat. The voice responds, "What God has made clean, you must not call profane." Ostensibly, the vision is about food, but it's really about human beings. We know this because there is a knock at the door, messengers from the household of Cornelius, a Gentile, looking for Peter. Peter goes with the messengers to proclaim, for the first time, the good news of Jesus to the Gentiles. Taking the point of his vision on the rooftop, Peter opens his sermon with these words: "I truly understand that God shows no partiality." The mystical experience Peter had on the rooftop had dismantled his prejudice. This was an apocalypse for Peter, a revelation about how God embraced all of humanity. In a similar way, much like what happened to Thomas Merton on Fourth and Walnut, we have experiences with God that explode our hearts and expand them with love. As Merton shared, looking at the strangers passing him on the street, "I was suddenly overwhelmed with the realization that I loved all those people." Like the Grinch in Dr. Seuss's *How the Grinch Stole Christmas*, we find our hearts growing "three sizes," flooded and filled with an affection that we did not previously possess. Love is given to us as a gift.

Assurance, mission, and conviction. Walking through these religious experiences in the Bible and in our lives illustrates the diversity of the perceptions and insights that are graced to us. If we widen our view about what a mystical experience might feel like, my hunch is that if we inventory our lives, we've had many such moments. Our hearts have been "strangely warmed" by the love of God. God has placed things in our hearts and called us to some work, even if it's just showing up on the doorstep with a casserole or being kinder to a coworker. And like Peter on the rooftop, God has convicted us of our failings, how we've not loved a certain group of people or a particular person as much as we should have. The list goes on and on.

Turns out, if we bring a little willingness to see, we've been bumping into God our entire lives. We've just been too distracted to notice, too busy to stop and pay attention. Too hurried to say, "Here am I. Send me." As Jesus said over and over again in the gospels, "Whoever has ears, let them hear." Like Johnny Cash in Nickajack Cave, God is whispering to us, "I am still here."

5

LIVING IN A ONE-STORY UNIVERSE

I was recently invited to address the graduating nursing students at my college. The talk was for their pinning ceremony. A beloved tradition in the nursing profession going back to Florence Nightingale, the ceremony welcomes new nurses to the profession as they are given a pin from their school.

I shared with the soon-to-be pinned nurses that, in the midst of the very busy days ahead of them, wherever their practices should take them, they would be standing on holy ground. Nurses are regularly around whenever our bodies and spirits have been pushed to their limits, where life regularly rubs elbows with death. God shows up in those places, in the courage, the grace, the sorrow, the hope, the loss, and the love. Nurses bear witness to it all. But if you're not paying attention, I said to the graduates, you're going to miss these sacred moments. You'll be too distracted by all the things you have to do during your shift or too checked out doing a procedure you've done a million times before. Which happens to all of us, no matter our jobs. "So open your eyes," I implored. "You will be standing at the crossroads of body and soul, life and death, joy and grief. So don't miss a thing. Bear witness." I read to the nurses the quote I shared earlier from Marilynne Robinson: "It has seemed to me sometimes as though the Lord breathes on this poor gray ember of Creation and it turns to radiance—for a moment or a year or the span of a life. And then it sinks back into itself again, and to look at it no one would know it had anything to do with fire, or light." "Your days are going to burn like fire," I told the nurses. "May your eyes and hearts be open."

One of my favorite works of art is a statue on my campus. If you are ever in West Texas, take a moment to visit *Jacob's Dream* here in Abilene. A sculpture by Jack Maxwell, *Jacob's Dream* depicts the story from Genesis 28. A stunning piece of art, *Jacob's Dream* is set in a stone grotto, with the main sculpture soaring into the sky depicting four massive angels climbing a ladder toward the heavens.

You likely recall the story from Genesis that inspired Jack's sculpture. Jacob is on the run from his brother Esau, and he finds himself in the desert out in the middle of nowhere. When night comes, Jacob falls asleep and has a dream. In the dream, he has a vision of a ladder, reaching from heaven to earth, with angels ascending and descending upon it. Upon waking, Jacob declares, "Surely the Lord is in this place—and I did not know it! How awesome is this place! This is none other than the house of God, and this is the gate of heaven." Jacob takes a stone to mark where his head rested during the night, anointing and consecrating the place. He names the spot "Bethel," meaning the "House of God."

Recovering enchantment is learning to see the world like Jacob. That is what I was trying to share with the nursing students. The gate of heaven could be anywhere, and it often shows up unexpectedly and in the middle of nowhere special. There we are, stressed or bored in the midst of a routine workday, and suddenly God breathes upon the cold ember of our life, and it all turns to fire. You find yourself standing at the gateway to heaven.

But too many Christians are living like atheists, operating as if God doesn't exist. We don't expect to bump into God around the watercooler or doing the dishes. We might *believe* in God, but we don't expect to *encounter* God. We're not going through the day with the eyes of Jacob, on the lookout for the gateway of heaven.

Christians live like atheists, according to the Orthodox priest and author Stephen Freeman, because we think we're living in a two-story universe. In this two-story universe, the cosmos is a house with two floors. As Freeman describes it, "We live here on earth, the first floor, where things are simply things and everything operates according to normal, natural laws, while God lives in heaven, upstairs, and is largely removed from the story in which we live. To effect anything here, God must interrupt the laws of nature and perform a miracle." For us to see or hear from God, God has to come downstairs to visit us. But most of the time, it's just us alone on the first floor. God is absent, upstairs and minding his own business.

When we live our lives in the two-story world, we practice what Freeman calls "Christian atheism." Since God is "upstairs," God is "not here." God isn't close; God is elsewhere, far away and distant. And not just physically distant, mentally distant as well. God is at the back our minds, an afterthought, if we think of God at all.

What we need to recover, according to Freeman, is a one-story vision of the universe. We need to see that God is, in the words of Freeman, "everywhere present and filling all things." In a one-story view of the universe, God and humanity are all living on the same floor. We're roommates with God and expect to see each other all the time. Like Jacob declared, we're living in the house of God.

Theologians have a fancy name for this one-story view of the world. They call it a "sacramental ontology."

Ontology is concerned with "existence," our thoughts and ideas about "reality." A good definition of *sacrament* is "a visible sign of an invisible reality." Putting the two together, "sacramental ontology" is about how everything around us, everything that exists, points us toward God. All the world is a sign.

But that's not quite right. Sacraments are more than signs. There's a famous story about Flannery O'Connor, the Catholic author who wrote such strange and startling stories about the Protestant South. O'Connor was a very devout Catholic, and she once found herself at a dinner party in New York City, hobnobbing with artists, writers, and literary critics. During the gathering, the topic of the Eucharist came up. The skeptics in the group assumed that Flannery, being the only Catholic in attendance, would defend the sacrament. Mary McCarthy, a writer and essayist, added her two cents, quipping that she though the Eucharist was a beautiful "symbol." To which O'Connor replied, "Well, if it's a symbol, to hell with it."

As we've noted, O'Connor's remark speaks to how, after the Protestant Reformation, the Eucharist became disenchanted. For Mary McCarthy and many Protestants, the Eucharist is just a sign, the bread and wine functioning as symbols that point our minds toward Jesus. But for Catholics like Flannery O'Connor, the Eucharist is more than a sign and symbol. The Eucharist is a miracle, an enchantment, the mystical transformation of the bread

and wine into the body and blood of Jesus. And according to O'Connor, without that miracle, the Eucharist was
useless.

So sacraments are more than signs. If sacraments are
merely signs, we're back to living in the two-story universe, with the downstairs "sign" pointing toward an
upstairs "reality." But as Flannery O'Connor teaches us,
sacraments *participate* in and *embody* the spiritual reality
they symbolize. Sacraments bring the miracle close. As
Catholics say about the Eucharist, God is "really present"
in the sacrament, *in the same room with us,* and not just
observing us from the upstairs. A sacramental ontology
expands this vision, coming to see God as "really present" in all things and everywhere in the world. Again, as
Gerard Manley Hopkins wrote, "The world is charged
with the grandeur of God." God's vitality and life crackle
through nature like spiritual electricity. The sunlight, the
wind, and the rain are not just signs pointing us toward
the Creator. God is "really present" in nature. God is
embracing us in the sunlight on our face, the raindrops on
our skin, and the breeze in our hair. God comes to us in
people as well. As Hopkins wrote in a different poem,
"Christ plays in ten thousand places, lovely in limbs, and
lovely in eyes not his." God is really present in the faces
and hands of other human beings as we love each other.

This sacramental ontology shows up all over the Bible. My favorite example comes from Acts 14, the first sermon in the history of the world preached to a wholly pagan audience. In the first thirteen chapters of Acts, which recounts the growth and missionary efforts of the early church, the sermons sound very much the same. Delivered to fellow Jews and God-fearing Gentiles, the first gospel preachers could rely on a shared history with their audience, their common experience with the God of Abraham, Isaac, and Jacob. But in Acts 14, Paul and Barnabas, traveling through the cities around the Mediterranean Sea, have been rejected at Jewish synagogues. So they turn their attention to the Gentiles of the city, a pagan audience.

In Acts 14, after healing a lame man, a crowd gathers, and Paul delivers a sermon. But no one in Paul's audience that day knew anything about the ten plagues or the Ten Commandments. Lacking a shared religious history with his listeners, Paul faced a challenge. How do you introduce and describe God—the God who has lived in the same room with you your entire life—to a people who have never seen or heard of him before? Here's what Paul said: "Friends . . . we bring you good news, that you should turn from these worthless things to the living God, who made the heaven and the earth and the sea and all that is in them. In past generations he allowed all the nations to follow their own ways; yet he has not left himself without a witness in doing good—giving you rains from heaven and fruitful seasons, and filling you with food and your hearts with joy." Unable to appeal to Abraham or Moses, Paul turns the attention of his audience to the natural world. God is "everywhere present" in this one-story world. Just like a roommate, God has always been speaking to us. As Paul says, "He has not left himself without witness." God's voice is heard in the rain and in the harvest. God is close where there is good food and the laugher of friends. God has been with you this entire time, declares Paul, "filling your hearts with joy." Start with joy if you're looking for enchantment. Let gladness be your guide to the gateway of heaven.

Recovering this sacramental ontology is the next big step toward enchanting our faith in this skeptical age. This is a one-story universe. So let's stop going through the day living as if God doesn't exist. God is everywhere present. God isn't that mysterious neighbor living in the apartment above you. God is closer than you can imagine. The signs and sacraments are all around you. Christ is playing in ten thousand places. The world hums with sacred electricity. Listen for the laughter and follow your joy. You are standing at the gateway to heaven. You are living in the House of God.

6

THE GOOD
CATASTROPHE

Elves and prisons might not seem like they go together,
but one of the reasons I've become so convicted about our
need for enchantment comes from what I've witnessed
leading a Bible study in a maximum-security prison.

In 1939, J. R. R. Tolkien, spinner of tales about wizards and dragons as the author of *The Hobbit* and *The Lord
of the Rings*, delivered a lecture in St Andrews, Scotland.
The talk, later published as "On Fairy-Stories," shares
Tolkien's reasons for why "fairy stories" are important.
According to Tolkien, fairy stories aren't silly entertain-
ments intended only for children. Fairy stories are serious, adult business. And for the inmates in my Bible
study, fairy stories are a matter of life and death.

Tales of fantasy and enchanted lands—what Tolkien calls "fairy stories"—strike us as examples of escape, pretend, and "make-believe." It's rousing fun to experience, in book or film, Bilbo's confrontation with Smaug the Dragon in *The Hobbit* or the terror of the Mines of Moria with the wizard Gandalf in *The Lord of the Rings*. But after the story or movie is over, we put the book down or walk out of the theater to face the "real world." Fairy stories aren't "true"; they are imaginative fictions. Such is our attitude toward enchantment. Enchantment is childish, make-believe, and wishful thinking. No serious adult believes in fairies, elves, and dragons. Skeptics direct the same attitude toward God as well.

But in "On Fairy-Stories," Tolkien tells us that the power of these tales isn't that they are "make-believe." Fairy stories are practices of seeing and attention, training ourselves in attitudes of perception. As I hope to show you, fairy stories help us assume a particular posture toward the world and our lives. Believing in elves isn't what's helpful to the men in prison. But what is absolutely critical for their mental and spiritual well-being is the posture fairy stories so wonderfully illustrate and help us practice. We've described this posture as "eccentric," an outward turn looking beyond ourselves and present circumstances. This is what the men in my Bible study so desperately need, an outward turn toward grace, help, hope, and a conviction of worthiness that comes to them from beyond the ruin of their lives and the confines of their prison cell. You and I need this outward turn as well. Our health and happiness depend upon it.

I don't know if you've noticed, but life in the "real world" is often burdened by boredom and weariness. We move numbly from workday to workday, entertainment to entertainment, screen to screen. Worst of all, our relationships become affected by a "taken for granted" feeling. We confess the tragedy of this, the monotony we feel with others, even with those we love most dearly. But we struggle to regain contact with wonder, surprise, and awe.

The enchantment of fairy stories, according to Tolkien, helps us recover these lost feelings. What was old becomes new. The boring becomes surprising. The gray becomes bright. The dead comes back to life again. What heals us in fairy stories, says Tolkien, is this sense of *recovery*. He writes, "Before we reach such states [like boredom and tedium] we need recovery. We should look at green again, and be startled anew. . . . We should meet the centaur and the dragon, and then perhaps suddenly behold, like the ancient shepherds, sheep, and dogs, and horses—and wolves. This recovery fairy-stories help us to make." Enchantment isn't "pretending," a fanciful fleeing or escaping the world. Enchantment is *rediscovering* the world. Enchantment isn't a flight but a return. Enchantment is looking at green again and being startled anew, seeing the world shine again like transfiguration. As Tolkien says, enchantment is "re-gaining the world," recovering "the queerness of things that have become trite, when they are seen suddenly from a new angle." Fairy stories help us recover our sacramental ontology, reminding us that we live in a one-story universe where God is everywhere present. Here's how "On Fairy-Stories" describes this recovery. It's a long paragraph, but it's so rich, I want to quote it in full:

> [Recovery] is a re-gaining—regaining of a clear view. I do not say "seeing things as they are" [but rather] "seeing things as we are (or were) meant to see them"—as things apart from ourselves. We need, in any case, to clean our windows; so that the things seen clearly may be freed from the drab blur of triteness or familiarity—from possessiveness. Of all faces those of our familiars are the ones both most difficult to play fantastic tricks with, and most difficult really to see with fresh attention, perceiving their likeness and unlikeness: that they are faces, and yet unique faces. This triteness is really the penalty of "appropriation": the things that are trite, or (in a bad sense) familiar, are the things that we have appropriated, legally or mentally. We say we know them. They have become like the things which once attracted us by their glitter, or their

color, or their shape, and we laid hands on them, and then locked them in our hoard, acquired them, and acquiring ceased to look at them.

There are many things to unpack here. To start, notice again how enchantment is fundamentally about perception. Tolkien calls it "cleaning our windows." This is especially important, as Tolkien points out, in how we see the faces of those we love most dearly. Enchantment isn't "seeing things as they are" but "seeing things as we are (or were) meant to see them." Enchantment isn't concerned with a *scientific description* of the world but with *beholding the sacred meaning* of the world. Enchantment is the daily work of "cleaning the dirty windows" of our perceptions so that the familiar surprises us again with joy, wonder, and gratitude. Suddenly, we are startled anew by the color green and feel a fresh surge of love gazing into the face of a loved one.

The windows of our perception become dirty when we own, master, and possess the world. Triteness, Tolkien says, is the penalty of appropriation, taking something as your own. Boredom is the price of possessiveness. Monotony is the cost of acquiring and hoarding. And the possessiveness here is fundamentally psychological in nature, assuming that we "know" this thing or person. This is how the detached, objective scientific gaze can become so diabolical. When we "know" something, it loses its capacity to surprise and startle us. Life becomes factual and "objectified," stripped of its magic and mystery. As Tolkien says, "the things which once attracted us by their glitter, or their color, or their shape" lost their magic when "we laid hands on them, and then locked them in our hoard." And in doing so, we "ceased to look." We lost our willingness to see.

The enchantment we recover in fairy stories battles against the deadness of the scientific gaze. In fairy stories, we recover the world as "a thing apart from ourselves," as hallowed and sacred, as something we cannot master, something mysterious, strange, and wonderful. And if that stance strikes us as "childlike," it's because children remain surprised by the world, experiencing it as magical and miraculous. For Tolkien, enchantment is simply "the wonder of the things, such as stone, and wood, and iron; tree and grass; house and fire; bread and wine." We crave this sacramental experience of the world, where common and ordinary things become symbols and signposts, inbreakings of the divine, and gateways to heaven. Sacramental wonder might be childlike, but let's not forget the words of Jesus: "You must become like little children to enter the kingdom of heaven."

Beyond recovering sacramental wonder, fairy stories help us look hopefully to the horizon for help and rescue. Fairy stories remind us of the eccentric shape of our lives, of our need for the outward turn. As Dietrich Bon-hoeffer so aptly summed it up, "Help must come from the outside."

Tolkien calls this aspect of fairy stories "consolation." For Tolkien, consolation is the very essence of enchantment, the "highest function" of the fairy story. This aspect of fairy stories is so important and so vital, Tolkien coined a word to name it. The Greek word *katastrophe* means "a sudden turn," and it's where we get the word *catastrophe*, a "sudden turn" for the worse. But where a tragic story is built around a final, bitter, hopeless catastrophe, the fairy story points in the opposite direction, toward a surprising, unexpected *rescue*. To name this feature of fairy stories, Tolkien affixed the Greek prefix *eu-* for "good" to the "sudden turn," creating the word *eucatastrophe*. The eucatastrophe is the "good catastrophe." In the words of Tolkien, the good catastrophe is "the sudden joyous 'turn,'" which is an experience of "sudden and miraculous grace."

Lest this be mistaken for wishful thinking, our hope for the eucatastrophe is not a denial of the sorrows and sufferings of the world. The eucatastrophe is a commitment to hope—loyalty and fidelity to hope. As Tolkien comments, the eucatastrophe "does not deny the existence of dyscatastrophe, of sorrow and failure." Rather, as loyalty to hope, the eucatastrophe "denies (in the face of much evidence, if you will) universal final defeat." In the midst of the darkness, the eucatastrophe is the herald of a coming dawn, a vision that gives us "a fleeting glimpse of Joy," a "Joy beyond the walls of the world."

If you're tempted to think that this hope is merely the childish longing for a "happily ever after" ending, let's return to Auschwitz and the observations of Viktor Frankl in *Man's Search for Meaning*. Don't imagine for an instant that the eucatastrophe is the stuff of children and gullible adults. Hope is a matter of life and death. Remember the question Frankl asked in the Nazi death camps. How are human beings able to carry on, day after day, in the face of a brutal, dehumanizing existence? Here's what Frankl observed about the eucatastrophe in *Man's Search for Meaning*:

> The prisoner who had lost his faith in the future—his future—was doomed. With his loss of belief in the future, he also lost his spiritual hold; he let himself decline and became subject to mental and physical decay. Usually this happened quite suddenly, in the form of a crisis, the symptoms of which were familiar to the experienced camp inmate. . . . Usually it began with the prisoner refusing one morning to get dressed and wash or to go out on the parade grounds. No entreaties, no blows, no threats had any effect.

He just lay there, hardly moving. If this crisis was brought about by an illness, he refused to be taken to the sick-bay or to do anything to help himself. He simply gave up.

I see this play out every week in the prison where I lead a Bible study. Many of the men I spend time with in the prison find themselves in very hopeless situations—facing life without parole or mandatory sentences lasting decades. How can they keep on living, day after day?

The answer comes in the eucatastrophe, in the eccentric posture where we look for a strength and courage that comes to us from beyond the horizon of our present, troubled circumstances. Just like what happens in Ezekiel. In Ezekiel 37, the prophet finds himself in a Valley of Dry Bones. After touring the bones, the Lord asks Ezekiel, "Mortal, can these bones live?" This is the question the men face in prison. Is there any hope for me? After the mess I've made of my life, is there any point in going on? Over and over, the men in the prison face God's question: Can these bones live?

The eucatastrophe is the only possible answer to that question. Within the Valley of Dry Bones, there is no potential, no options, no answers. In the Valley of Dry Bones, there is only fatalism and resignation. Hope has to come to us *eccentrically*, from the *outside*, from somewhere *beyond* the valley. And that is what happens in Ezekiel 37.

The Spirit of God brings "the sudden turn," blowing over the dead bones and bringing them back to life.

Let me be clear about what is happening here. The experience of eucatastrophe in the prison—God breathing life back into the dead—isn't the naive belief that tomorrow you'll be released from prison. The eucatastrophe is, instead, the steady conviction that a rich and meaningful life is possible, that God still has plans for you, that life is worth living. This conviction comes from the outside because the meaning and value the men in prison discover *transcend* their objective circumstances. Hope doesn't spring from logical, scientific, and rational deductions about the "facts." Science is useless in the Valley of Dry Bones. I love a good space documentary as much as the next person, but quasars and black holes, as wondrous as they are, provide zero hope to the men in prison. Facts are dry bones. The men in my Bible study are facing years upon years, perhaps the rest of their life, behind bars. Those are the facts. The eucatastrophe tells them why life is worth living *in spite of the facts.* Hope comes from the outside.

This is why the eucatastrophe, as the fairy story reminds us, is an experience of enchantment. Hope has an eccentric shape. Hope transcends the facts and looks toward the grace that saves us from the outside. And this isn't wishful thinking or make-believe. As Frankl observed in Auschwitz and I do in the prison, hope is a matter of life and death.

"Rejoice in the Lord always: and again I say, Rejoice."

Hope isn't the only symptom of this eccentric posture; joy is as well.

In Philippians, the apostle Paul mentions "joy" or "rejoice" sixteen times across 106 verses. Paul's short letter to the church in Philippi overflows with delight and jubilation. Because of this, Philippians is often described as Paul's "Epistle of Joy."

What's fascinating about this is that Philippians is also one of Paul's prison letters. The guy who wrote "Rejoice in the Lord always!" wasn't skiing on a mountain or sipping Coronas by the pool. Paul wasn't sitting in his cozy little reading nook with a warm cup of tea, curated for that Instagram-worthy moment. Paul was in jail. And in the trouble and darkness, Paul was bubbling over with joy.

I expect all of us would like to know the secret of Paul's durable, steady, and courageous happiness.

The secret is the same one we observed with hope. Joy comes to us eccentrically, from the outside, from beyond our present, dismal circumstances.

Paul himself describes it as "the secret." As he shares with the Philippians, "I have learned to be content with whatever I have. I know what it is to have little, and I know what it is to have plenty. In any and all circumstances I have learned the secret of being well-fed and of going hungry, of having plenty and of being in need" (Philippians 4:11–12). The facts don't matter to Paul. Sometimes he's well fed, and sometimes he's hungry. But joy remains constant, transcending the facts, present no matter the situation.

What makes this possible, Paul shares, is the eucatastrophe, the eccentric nature of "the secret": "I can do all things through Christ who strengthens me." Joy isn't found within but *beyond* ourselves. Joy, if it is to be steady and constant, has to come to us from a Source outside of ourselves. Joy doesn't bubble up from a cold, logical appraisal of "the facts." The facts of life are a rollercoaster ride, sometimes up and sometimes down. So that is Paul's secret. Just like hope, joy has this eccentric, enchanted shape. Sitting in prison, Paul finds himself in the Valley of Dry Bones. But the Spirit of Jesus breathes life into Paul, filling him with joy. Experiencing the eucatastrophe, Paul shouts, "Rejoice!"

Beyond hope and joy, gratitude also has an eccentric shape. This is hugely important because gratitude is a defining characteristic of the happiest people in the world. It's not hard to see why. As we've noted, the Greek word *charis*, translated as "grace" in the Bible, is the same word for "gift." When we say "Thank you," psychological magic happens: life is transformed into an experience of grace. I observe this every week out at the prison. The most resilient men are those who continue to express gratitude, to experience life as a gift, even in the midst of their difficult circumstances.

If you doubt the transformative power of gratitude, try this experiment. Pick anything in your life that is a source of dissatisfaction. Maybe it's your old smartphone with its bad battery, your junky car, or a less-than-satisfying job. Now make it a practice over the next few days to express heartfelt thanks for your phone, car, job, or anything else in your life. Be thankful that you have a phone, or a car, or a job. Millions of people don't have any of these things. So take time this week, as the old hymn exhorts, to "count your blessings."

Then sit back and watch the psychological magic do its work. Notice, when you count your blessings, how a source of dissatisfaction is transformed into a location of joy. Now imagine extending this thankfulness across every sphere of your life. Imagine what it would be like to experience everything in life—every moment, every possession, every task, every relationship—as gift and grace. It would be absolutely transformative. No wonder gratitude makes people happy.

You can see the eccentric shape of gratitude at work when you notice how nothing really changes, factually speaking, when you express gratitude for your junky old smartphone. The facts about the phone remain the same; its battery life is still abysmal. But in expressing thanks, the phone becomes an experience of grace. This is a pattern that should be getting familiar. Hope, joy, and gratitude keep pushing us beyond the facts, turning us outward, looking for a grace that originates beyond ourselves.

Gratitude has this eccentric shape because it is a *social* and *relational* emotion, the positive feelings we experience when we've been given a gift or favor. Gifts imply a giver. So when we feel grateful for the beauty of nature and for life itself, our feelings (if not our minds) assume we're in a *personal relationship* with the cosmos. Our emotions assume a Gift Giver. Of course, feeling grateful for the world and life isn't a logical proof that a gift-giving Creator exists. But as a social emotion in response to a gift, gratitude puts us in an enchanted posture. You can't be grateful for existence and be an atheist at the same time, at least not emotionally. Gratitude is a posture of prayer. Gratitude is giving thanks.

If you doubt this, consider how gratitude cannot exist in a wholly materialistic cosmos. If cosmic history is simply the deterministic or probabilistic unfolding of the laws of physics, there is no gift to be experienced here. At best, we can feel *fortunate* and *lucky* in a wholly materialistic cosmos. As the scientists never tire of telling us, we're all quite lucky to be here. If the earth was a little closer or farther away from the sun, I wouldn't be here to type these words, and you wouldn't be around to read them. Thinking about that makes me feel very, very lucky. But feeling lucky isn't the same as feeling grateful. It's one thing to feel like you've dodged a cosmic bullet to the head and quite another to receive your life as a gift.

And unlike gratitude, feeling lucky isn't a foundation of emotional and mental health. In fact, feeling lucky can cut in the opposite direction. Perhaps we really did win the cosmic lottery, the odds of life emerging in our solar system astronomically small. Given those long odds, most of us feel fortunate about our lives, feelings that can be leveraged into a moral response. Life is precious and rare, the scientists tell us, so we should protect and cherish it. And we should. But not everyone experiences the cosmic lottery this way. If life was wildly improbable, a lucky throw of the dice, a cosmic accident, then life might not have any purpose or meaning at all. The silent, indifferent cosmos doesn't care about the small, private dramas of my life. Looking at the vast, cold universe, billions of years old, our lives can feel diminished, useless, and pointless. The existential philosopher Jean-Paul Sartre set it out plainly: "Every existing thing is born without reason, prolongs itself out of weakness and dies by chance." Them's the facts in a wholly materialistic cosmos. Which is why a purely materialistic account of life is inherently nihilistic and inhuman. As the Nobel-laureate physicist and atheist Steven Weinberg confessed about the fruits of a wholly scientific view of the cosmos, "The more the universe seems comprehensible, the more it also seems pointless." True, few of us feel this way about being a cosmic accident, that our lives are pointless, but some of us do. Regardless, the thing to note is how feeling lucky always has this potential to tip into despair. Gratitude, by contrast, causes us to feel blessed and graced, welcome and at home in the universe. You are not a cosmic accident; you were *meant* to be here. The cosmic security of this enchantment provides us with a firm, steady platform for happiness and joy. All of life is a gift. And we give thanks. Help keeps coming to us from the outside.

A final way the eucatastrophe shows up in prison, help coming to us from the outside, is in the inmates' struggle for value, worth, and dignity. As you can imagine, shame is crippling inside a prison. Given the mistakes the men have made, they are tempted to see themselves as worthless and devoid of value. And society does all it can to treat the incarcerated as trash, as stored human waste. In the face of those facts, value and worth must come to the men eccentrically, as a gift that transcends their shame and the stigma of society.

We all need the eccentric gift of worthiness. Trouble is, our culture keeps turning us inward, telling us that *self-esteem* is the pathway to mental health. We're told that cultivating a healthy self-esteem is critical to emotional well-being. So we try to instill self-esteem in our children, our loved ones, and ourselves, attempting to nurture a healthy self-concept.

But let me ask you some questions: How's this working out for you? How healthy is your self-esteem? What about your children and loved ones? How are they feeling about themselves? The data here is pretty clear. While America is the most affluent nation in the history of the world, our rates of anxiety, depression, suicide, and addiction are all skyrocketing. We're not doing very well. We are a deeply unwell society.

What's gone wrong is that the marketed cure is a poison. Our problem is self-esteem. Because at its heart, self-esteem is an *evaluation*: How am I measuring up? We answer this question in one of two ways. First, we compare ourselves to others. Am I as thin as Mariah? Do I make as much money as Anthony? Is our marriage as happy as Blair and Jordan's? And so on. This is why social media is such a curse. Through Facebook and Instagram, we compare our sad lives to the curated images of happiness from our friends, family, and coworkers, triggering massive amounts of envy and dissatisfaction. Our lives don't measure up.

Second, when we're not comparing ourselves to the lives of others, we judge our self-esteem by assessing our performance in meeting our goals and expectations. Way back in 1890, in the very first psychology textbook published in America, William James defined self-esteem as the ratio of our successes to our aspirations. Self-esteem informs you, emotionally, how successful you have been in reaching the goals you've set for your life. If you're achieving your goals, you feel increased self-esteem. If you're falling short of the life you want for yourself, you experience lower self-esteem.

Few of us, though, have the life we've desired, planned, or dreamed for, at least not 100 percent of that life. Most of us are living with unfulfilled or even broken dreams. Life hasn't quite turned out the way we planned, not completely. So we experience all the symptoms of low self-esteem: depression, anxiety, feelings of inadequacy, shame, envy, and resentment.

Stepping back, it's really no wonder we're all so unhealthy and unhappy. We've told ourselves that a healthy self-esteem is the surest route to happiness, but self-esteem is rooted in evaluation, comparison, and performance. Linking our psychological health to our ability to compare well to others and succeed has been a complete disaster. Our emotional well-being has become a tragic roller-coaster ride. We feel good about ourselves when things are going well but fall into depression when things are not. We're up, and then we're down. Self-esteem isn't a thermostat, set and steady; it's a thermometer, rising and falling in response to the events in our lives. And just imagine what it would be like trying to secure self-esteem if you found yourself in prison carrying a life sentence without parole. It seems pretty clear: self-esteem can never be a stable and durable foundation for joy. If we're building our happiness on self-esteem, we're building that house on a foundation of sand.

What we all need—you and I and the men in my Bible study—is a source of value that is durable, consistent, and unconditional. We need to experience our lives and actions as significant and valuable regardless of situation and circumstance. As we've learned, psychologists have a name for this; it's called *mattering*, the steady conviction that your life and actions have value regardless of present circumstances. Mattering allows our value to escape the trap of self-esteem, swinging between its highs and lows. You matter—your life has value and significance—when you get the promotion and when you don't. You matter no matter your weight, romantic situation, employment, or income. You matter in prison, in your failure, and in your mistakes. You matter, no matter what.

Mattering is an enchantment because it comes to us from beyond a purely materialistic, factual, and scientific account of our lives. Mattering isn't a measurement, and it's not an evaluation. Mattering isn't a trophy that you can win or lose. You don't perform for it and you cannot earn it. Mattering is a gift. That's its power and what makes it steady and unshakable. We *matter* because of *grace*. That's good news for the men in my Bible study. Enchantment has saved their lives. It can save yours as well. Grace is the only thing in the world that is stronger than shame.

A wonderful example of mattering as grace comes from Howard Thurman in *Jesus and the Disinherited*, a book that had a profound impact upon Martin Luther King Jr. Thurman explores why Black people in the United States were attracted to Christianity, to Jesus in particular. What did the slaves find attractive about Jesus? According to Thurman, it was mattering. The facts of slavery couldn't have been more bleak and painful. How can a person be expected to develop a "healthy self-esteem" in such inhuman and dehumanizing conditions? Dignity doesn't emerge from "the facts," because "the facts" are telling you you're inferior. Dignity must come to us eccentrically, religiously, from the outside. And this, says Thurman, is exactly why slaves were so attracted to Jesus. Jesus told them they mattered. Jesus was their eucatastrophe, the help that came to them from the outside. Here is Thurman describing the eccentric nature of dignity and mattering and its impact upon the mental health of the disadvantaged and oppressed:

> The core of the analysis of Jesus is that man is a child of God. . . . This idea—that God is mindful of the individual—is of tremendous import. . . . In this world the socially disadvantaged man is constantly given a negative answer to the most important personal questions upon which mental health depends: "Who am I? What am I?"

The first question has to do with a basic self-estimate, a profound sense of belonging, of counting. If a man feels that he does not belong in a way in which it is perfectly normal for others to belong, then he develops a deep sense of insecurity. When this happens to a person, it provides the basic material for what the psychologist calls the inferiority complex. It is quite possible for a man to have no sense of personal inferiority as such, but at the same time to be dogged by a sense of social inferiority. The awareness of being a child of God tends to stabilize the ego and results in a new courage, fearlessness, and power. I have seen it happen again and again.

[Seeing oneself as a child of God establishes] the ground of personal dignity, so that a profound sense of personal worth can absorb the fear reaction. This alone is not enough, but without it, nothing else is of value. The first task is to get the self immunized against the most radical results of the threat of violence. When this is accomplished, relaxation takes the place of churning fear. The individual now feels that he counts, that he belongs.

Mental health requires a rock-solid conviction that you count; that you belong; that nothing, not even being a slave, can deprive you of your birthright; that you are a beloved child of God. And this isn't a therapeutic issue, not really. Slaves don't need counseling or antidepressants. Dignity is an enchantment, a religious conviction. Shame is a religious problem. Do you *believe* you matter? Because at the end of the day, our worth is simply a gift we have to receive. Mattering is grace. This is the enchantment that guards our hearts and minds, buffering us from failure and shame. Just as it protected, like a fierce guardian angel, the mental health of Black people during the dark generations as they endured slavery and segregation.

Enchantment continues to ground and guard the value of oppressed and marginalized people. This is what struck me reading Chris Arnade's book *Dignity: Seeking Respect in Back Row America*. In the book, Arnade, a nonbeliever, takes a tour through rural and inner-city America, spending time with and interviewing the people on the economic margins of society, the people left behind by the American dream. What Arnade discovered about faith and dignity among the poor revolutionized his view of religion. Prior to his tour of back-row America, Arnade, who was trained as a scientist, embraced the elite consensus of our skeptical age, that religion is just a bunch of superstitions, myths, and fairy tales. As Arnade describes,

> When I went into graduate school for physics I spent six years studying the big questions—how

the universe started, what it was made of, and what is our place in it. I embraced the belief that humans can understand and figure out our world, and that there was no question too big that we couldn't solve, accepting an implicit arrogance in mankind's ability to rise above our surroundings. . . .

I was not alone. Most of us in the front row [the wealthy, privileged parts of America] had decided that it was impossible to identify absolutes, that any moral certainties in religion were suspect, and that all we could know or value was what science revealed to be quantifiable. Religion was often seen as an old, irrational thing that limited and repressed people.

But as Arnade toured back-row America, talking and listening to people in poor rural and inner-city communities, he kept following his new acquaintances into churches. What he discovered there, sitting in the pews and folding chairs of churches, is that science simply can't help us the way faith can when it comes to mattering, dignity, and mental health. Arnade discovered what Howard Thurman observed about the attraction of Jesus for the disadvantaged and oppressed. He continues,

Yet over the years I kept finding myself in churches, as I kept finding myself in McDonald's,

going there for one reason: because the people I
wanted to learn from spent their time there.

Often the only places open, welcoming,
and busy in back row neighborhoods were
churches and McDonald's. Often the people
using McDonald's were the same people using
the churches, people who sat for hours reading
or studying the Bible at a table or a booth. . . .

This is how it is on the streets. Faith is the
reality and the source of hope. Science is the distant thing that doesn't necessarily do much for
you.

When you live in back-row America, where every
social and economic metric points toward your low status and inferiority, it's pretty hard to develop a "healthy
self-esteem." Mattering has to come to us as a gift, as an
experience of grace. And science, as wonderful as it may
be, just doesn't traffic in grace.

My favorite story of grace and mattering in *Dignity*
comes from a story Arnade shares about Takeesha, a
prostitute Arnade interviewed in New York:

Takeesha was standing alone by a trickling
fire hydrant, washing her face. She was working, wearing thigh-high faux-leather red boots,
leopard-print pants, waving at whatever car or

truck passed by. I had seen her before, and she had always smiled at me or waved. . . .

We talked, and over the next half hour she told me her life story. She told me how her mother's pimp put her out on the streets at twelve. How she had her first child at thirteen. How she was addicted to heroin. I ended by asking her the question I asked everyone I photographed: "How do you want to be described?" She replied without a pause, "As who I am. A prostitute, a mother of six, and a child of God."

This is the enchantment of mattering, the religious solution to dignity and mental health. No matter your circumstances, even if you're sitting on the very back row of the American dream, you matter; you have value, worth, and dignity. You are a child of God.

The point of fairy stories isn't to force yourself to believe in elves and dragons. What fairy stories dramatize is the eccentric shape of our lives. Fairy stories remind us, in whimsical ways, of a life-giving and lifesaving truth: that wonder, hope, joy, gratitude, and dignity are found in the good catastrophe, in a recovery of the world, and in a grace that comes to us from the outside. In this skeptical age, fairy stories are resistance literature, pointing us toward the spiritual revolution that will save our lives from boredom, deadness, hopelessness, dissatisfaction, nihilism, and despair.

So clean your windows. Take a look again at the world and see it, this time, the way you were meant to see it. Recover your sacramental wonder and be shocked anew by the color green. Become like a child and enter the kingdom of heaven. Count your blessings and rejoice. Always rejoice. Look to the horizon in hope, even in the Valley of Dry Bones. And remember why you matter. You are a child of God.

7

LIVE YOUR
BEAUTIFUL LIFE

Many years ago, a student of mine—I'll call him William—came to me in the midst of some faith struggles. The "New Atheists" were all the rage back then. You might remember them: Richard Dawkins, Christopher Hitchens, Sam Harris. Their book titles were dropping from the sky like metaphysical bombs: *The God Delusion*, *God Is Not Great*, and *The End of Faith*. William had read these books and found their arguments persuasive and unsettling. So we met for coffee and talked about all the issues he had questions about: evolution, the violence in the Old Testament, the problem of evil. It was a lovely conversation, and I tried to share the best of the Christian theological tradition in thinking about these questions.

Having tried my best to answer the many questions William had posed, toward the end of the conversation I asked William if I could ask him a question. "Of course," William agreed. So I asked, "William, do you want to live a beautiful life?"

That is a deep and profound question for our troubled, disenchanted hearts. Deeper than you might realize. We are ailing and feverish, and within the question I posed to William—"Do you want to live a beautiful life?"— medicine is being offered.

We live in a hope-sick world. We see this hope sickness everywhere. Hope is hard to come by, rare and diminishing. And as hope wanes, human flourishing wanes. Personally and collectively. Our emotional, social, and political lives are visibly sick, and much of our suffering is due to a loss of hope.

Consider how, in 2020, a new category of death was introduced by the economist Anne Case and Nobel Prize winner Angus Deaton. In their book, *Deaths of Despair and the Future of Capitalism*, Case and Deaton analyzed why life expectancies in the United States had fallen for three years successively for the first time since 1918. The cause was traced to a sharp uptick in what Case and Deaton have named "deaths of despair," deaths due to suicide, drug overdose, and liver disease resulting from alcoholism. In the United States, deaths of despair have been increasing over the last decade by 50 percent to over 300 percent, depending on the demographic group.

Hope sickness in our disenchanted world is also characterized by listlessness, boredom, and a felt sense of shallowness and flatness. We get lost in digital fogs for huge chunks of life—binging on Netflix and podcasts, playing video games, watching porn, and spending endless hours scrolling through social media. We also observe group identity fetishes surrounding brands and entertainment franchises, a world where *Star Wars* fans and video gamers send death threats to people who disturb their fan culture.

We see hope sickness in all of this because humans are teleological creatures. The word *teleological* comes from the Greek word *telos*, meaning "end." Teleology describes our ultimate end or aim. We are teleological creatures because we live *toward* the future. We live *for* something. We have goals and purposes in view. We have reasons for getting up in the morning and pushing through the day. But with the collapse of Christian belief in the West—in particular with our skepticism concerning heaven and an enchanted vision of our future—we've been left with a teleological vacuum. In our disenchanted age, we've lost the conviction that our lives have a goal and purpose, that we are heading somewhere. We used to look forward to heaven; now we look forward to the next Marvel movie.

Capitalism replaced heaven with an economy of *craving*—cravings that create future-oriented expectations. We look forward to some product about to hit the market or some film to arrive in the theaters. Consumerism hijacks our teleological hearts by placing new products in our future, giving us something to look forward to, something to live *for*. But the fake teleology of consumerism is haunted by boredom and shallowness. We scroll through social media like zombies. There are hundreds and hundreds of movies across all our streaming services, but we find nothing interesting to watch. I look forward to getting a new iPhone, but its better battery life doesn't heal the deep sadness in my life. Nor does a new Marvel or *Star Wars* release imbue my life with sacred weight and significance. Yes, we look forward to buying stuff and to movie releases, but life adrift in consumer and entertainment culture cannot satisfy our spiritual hungers and longings.

Capitalism also specializes in producing narcotizing products that take command of the serotonin and dopamine reward-pathways in the brain. Capitalism has demonstrated a vast capacity to anesthetize the world. As evidenced by rising deaths of despair, capitalism produces pain, but it also numbs it. You're being dissected alive on the surgical table, and you don't even notice.

Phrased differently, capitalism specializes in addiction, in targeting the pleasure, pain, and reward pathways of the brain. Consider all the ways the products of

capitalistic economies affect the dopaminergic and pleasure pathways of the brain:

- Sugar, fat, and salt (fast food, snack foods, sugary
  drinks)
- Video games (smartphone apps, PlayStation,
  Xbox)
- Sporting events (attending, watching, fantasy
  leagues)
- Gambling (online, casinos, lottery tickets)
- Caffeine
- Nicotine
- Alcohol
- Legalized marijuana
- Illegal drugs (opioids, meth, cocaine)
- TV and streaming services
- Movies
- Social media
- Widescreen TVs
- iPhones and smartphones
- Headphones
- Shopping (online and in person)

The list goes on and on. Everyone has their fix. My
poorer friends might live in squalor, but they have a
smartphone, a widescreen TV, an Xbox, Netflix, cig-
arettes, junk food, sugary drinks, lottery tickets, and
cheap beer. Beyond these, there is the temptation of

illegal drugs. That is a whole lot of pleasure—products that anesthetize dissatisfactions with the modern, disenchanted world.

My wealthier friends also have smartphones, on which they play games and surf social media. Their widescreen TVs are a part of a larger entertainment center. They drink bottles of wine, good whisky, and craft beer. Beyond Netflix, they also have Hulu, Disney+, AppleTV, Amazon Prime, and Paramount+. They wear AirPods or brand-name headphones to block out the world. Amazon Prime drops packages on the porch like Santa Claus. They also crave fat, salt, and sugar, but can afford upscale culinary experiences where food becomes art. They enjoy concerts, festivals, vacations, holidays, live sporting events, and traveling the world. And drug use haunts them as well.

Everyone has their fix. We live in a narcotized world. No matter your socioeconomic status, you can surround yourself with pleasures. A glass of wine or a cigarette. Stock trading or a lottery ticket. A football game or a Netflix binge. Instagram or chocolate. A video game or eBay. A trip to Italy or a music festival. It's really no surprise that people don't agitate for a better world. The fix is in, to shift the metaphor. We've buzzed, soothed, stimulated, and numbed our brains. We're rats in a cage, pushing the bar to get our next hit.

After decades of serving as a missionary in India, the famous missiologist Lesslie Newbigin returned to England in 1974. What Newbigin discovered upon his return home profoundly shocked him. The England Newbigin had left in the 1940s was a Christian nation. But during his long absence, the forces of secularism had overtaken the West and overwhelmed the church. Newbigin returned home to a disenchanted, post-Christian world.

Being a missiologist, Newbigin began to think about the cultural changes the West had undergone. How had England become disenchanted so quickly? Here's the question Newbigin asked: If visitors from ancient cultures were to visit modern England, what would strike them most forcefully? We might think it would be our technological prowess. Not so, argued Newbigin. What visitors from ancient cultures would most notice about the modern West, he said, is the fact/value split. Visitors from other cultures would be struck by how no one in the modern world can define what we mean by "good." And of all the cultures that have ever existed, this is a truly bizarre and unique feature. Until our time, every culture in the history of the world existed to tell you what was good and what was bad: These things are honorable and praiseworthy. These things are shameful and to be avoided. Such knowledge helped us skillfully navigate social life and honor our sacred duties. But our culture? We have a void. Where there should exist a shared vision of the good, we have an emptiness, a nothing, a nullity. We possess technology, but no shared vision of the true, the beautiful, and the good. And this, argued Newbigin, makes us a very strange people.

Let's look more closely at the modern split Newbigin observed between facts and values. On the one hand, there are facts—objective material realities discoverable through the empirical methods of scientific investigation. And then, on the other hand, there are values— judgments about goodness, moral truth, and beauty.

Prior to the Enlightenment, values were factual. Moral truths once were considered as factual as robins and rainbows. The verities of religious faith regarding the true, the beautiful, and the good were as obvious and reliable as the rising and setting of the sun. But in the wake of the Enlightenment, facts have become divorced from value. Scientific research can be used to reveal facts, but values, your beliefs and opinions about how to live your life, morally speaking—these are now up to you. And describing values as "beliefs" and "opinions" here is keenly diagnostic. In the modern world, values have lost their factual status and have been relegated to the private, subjective sphere, the realm of our personally held beliefs and opinions. We consider things like the reality of rocks and trees to be objective and universal, whereas values are considered subjective and personal. Values are not "real," and are now akin to lifestyle choices.

All this is important for our hope-sick world because the glue that once cemented facts to values was a teleological vision of the cosmos. This is the critical insight: *Teleology allows us to extract values from facts.* If we know what something is *for*, we can say whether something is *good.*

Consider a watch. What is a watch for? Well, a watch keeps the time; that's its function, its *telos*. And knowing the *telos* of the watch—its purpose—allows us to make value-based judgments given the facts of the watch. A "good" watch is a watch that keeps the time, fulfills its purpose. A "bad" watch doesn't keep the time. Notice here how values—judgments of good and bad—flow out of a factual description, how well the watch keeps time. What gives us this capacity to read values from facts is teleology, knowing the purpose, function, and *telos* of the watch.

With the rise of Newtonian mechanics, we jettisoned teleology for causality in how we viewed the cosmos. The universe was no longer understood as governed by higher purposes but was, rather, viewed as the product of a long chain of cause-and-effect. Where teleology looked to the future, causality looked to the past. And with this shift from teleology to causality, from an Aristotelian to a Newtonian picture of the world, the connection between facts and values was severed. Suddenly we could no longer say whether life was good because we no longer agreed on what life was *for*.

Everywhere we look we find evidence of our lost teleology. What is a human life for? What is the purpose of your life? Once upon a time, we had answers to such questions. For example, the Westminster Catechism, originally published in 1647, famously began with this teleological back-and-forth:

Question:
What is the purpose of man?

Answer:
The purpose of man is to glorify God and to enjoy him forever.

No matter what one might think of that answer, at least it was an answer. Life had a purpose, a *telos*, an end. And with that *telos* in hand, one could ask and answer questions regarding whether one was leading a good, true, and beautiful life. Lose this teleological vision and life becomes disenchanted and prone to both despair and addiction.

Understanding the relationship between teleology and enchantment is vital if we want to help our hope-sick world.

Over the last three decades, the field of positive psychology has turned its attention to examining variables such as happiness, gratitude, and joy. One of the most consistent findings from this research concerns how our overall well-being—emotional, physical, and relational—is related to having meaning in life. Living a meaningful life is associated with less depression, greater life satisfaction, and healthier behaviors, such as eating well and exercising. Meaning in life is a vital ingredient of "the Good Life."

As assessed by psychologists, meaning in life is a cord woven with three strands: coherence, purpose, and mattering. Coherence, or comprehension, involves the process of making sense of one's life. From a narrative perspective, coherence involves seeing one's life as a whole story woven together from one's experiences. When life doesn't make sense to us, or when a part of my life hasn't been incorporated into the narrative plot of my life, my lived experience feels disjointed and random. When life lacks coherence, we struggle to make sense of what has happened or is happening to us. Coherence is achieved when we feel that we "get" and understand our life story.

In addition to coherence, purpose in life involves having overarching goals that guide the direction of one's life. Purpose involves having a life "aim" that organizes our life goals and stimulates action. Where coherence is largely involved in meaning-making, purpose is motivational, catalyzing action and moving us toward what we deem the goal of our existence. Without purpose, life is experienced as drifting and directionless.

The final thread of meaning in life is existential mattering, also called significance. I described mattering in chapter 6. Mattering involves experiences of transcendent value and worth. When we matter, we experience life as worth living. Mattering is feeling that your life matters, no matter what. Which is to say, mattering is axiomatic, a non-negotiable given of your existence. Mattering has been contrasted with what is called contingent, or conditional, self-regard. Contingent self-regard places conditions upon self-worth and value: "I matter *if* . . ." You know the score: I matter *if* I am successful; I matter *if* I can lose twenty pounds; I matter *if* I get this job promotion. Mattering, as we've learned, is unconditional worth and value: your life matters regardless of your external circumstances of success or failure. Where self-esteem is often variable and fluctuating—that roller-coaster ride of pride and shame—mattering is steady and constant.

Coherence, purpose, and mattering are the three ingredients in living a meaningful life. What is fascinating to observe about the science of meaning of life is how it describes *a teleological posture* toward life. Well-being and happiness are associated with feeling that your life has a story (coherence), a story that is going somewhere (purpose), and a story that has cosmic, existential significance (mattering). Stated simply, we flourish when our hearts and minds operate teleologically. Joy flows out of story, purpose, and worth. Teleology is the medicine for our hope sickness.

Once upon a time, the Christian eschatological imagination provided us with the teleological framework on which happiness depends. *Eschatology* describes our beliefs about "the last things," where we think our lives are ultimately going. Christian eschatology provided us with hope. But we've turned our back on those beliefs, and deprived of that teleological vision, life now seems chaotic, directionless, and meaningless. A disenchanted, materialistic view of the cosmos reigns, granting us enormous technological prowess, but at great psychological and social cost. Facing the void, where the Christian eschatological imagination once provided us with story, purpose, and worth, the cosmos has become unintelligible. We sacrificed teleology for technology, and the universe is now experienced as having no meaning or direction at all. The famous French existentialist Albert Camus faced our modern vacuum of meaning in the opening lines of his book *The Myth of Sisyphus*: "There is only one really serious philosophical question, and that is suicide." Sisyphus, you'll recall from Greek mythology, was condemned by the gods to a punishment in the underworld where he had to roll a large rock up a hill, only to have it roll back down, over and over again. In comparing modern life to the fate of Sisyphus, Camus was wrestling with our lost teleology. Sisyphus is the perfect picture of an un-teleological life. Sisyphus's life *is going nowhere*, his exertions *leading nowhere*. And as Camus sees so clearly, *we* have become Sisyphus. With the loss of the Christian worldview, we now stand at the foot of the hill with Sisyphus. We've been stripped of story, purpose, and worth. We have lost our *telos*, our purpose. All our exertions are leading precisely *nowhere*. And so it's fair to ask, as Camus does, what makes such a life worth living?

William paused for a moment when I asked him if he wanted to live a beautiful life. He grew thoughtful, and then he answered, "Yes. I want to live a beautiful life." To which I said, "So do I. I want to live a beautiful life. But that raises a question for both of us: What do we find beautiful?"

I hope you can see what I was trying to share with William that day. I was asking William to think about his life teleologically and, by doing so, to step back into enchantment. I was asking William to overcome the fact/value split, the rip in the fabric of his life being forced upon him by the materialism of the New Atheists. I was asking William to consider the *purpose* of his life. Because you can only define a *beautiful* life if you know what life is *for*. I was asking William to walk toward meaning in life, inviting him into story, purpose, and worth. I was offering William medicine for his hope sickness. "You are not Sisyphus," I was saying to William with my question. "You are not condemned to a meaningless life. And you are not a drugged zombie of capitalism. Your life has a story, a story that is going somewhere, a story that matters. You can live a beautiful life."

So can you. And you live it by *practicing a rival teleological imagination* in this disenchanted world. That is how we step back into enchantment. For without this teleological orientation, we're doomed to hope sickness, despairing like Sisyphus or narcotized by the pain-numbing products of capitalism. Hope has to become an act of resistance in an age of despair and addiction. And lest anyone be confused, hope isn't about wishful thinking or a saccharine optimism tempting us into a cheerful, oblivious passivity. Hope activates and sustains our moral exertions. Hope is less about consolation than *motivation*.

Still, hope doesn't just happen by people telling each other, "Have hope!" Hope isn't a choice made at the sharp end of a command. Hope is a virtue, an emotional capacity we acquire through practice. Hope is a habit.

In the words of poet Wendell Berry, we must "practice resurrection."

There is a psychological concept, called "sanctification theory," that shows us how to do this. Sanctification theory illustrates how we can re-enchant our lives by practicing hope in a hope-sick world. Developed by psychologists Kenneth Pargament and Annette Mahoney, sanctification theory emerged from psychological research concerning goal-setting. As we know, goals fill our lives, structuring how we spend our time and energy. These goals range from the small to the large, from "I need to clean the toilet" to "I need to meet a critical deadline" to "I need to be a loving friend, spouse, or parent." Given the fact that goals have different priorities and values, we arrange our goals hierarchically. Less-valued goals are subordinated to higher, more-valued goals. This arrangement allows us to make decisions when goals come into conflict. All of this connects back to the research concerning meaning in life, as our life purpose is defined by our most-valued goals; indeed, a single overarching life aim functions as a master goal regulating all our other life goals. Everything works to serve this larger purpose in our life.

Pargament and Mahoney observed that some goals, along with our overarching life purpose, can become sanctified and enchanted. We sanctify and enchant goals by connecting them to some transcendent and sacred ground of meaning and value. For example, when I clean the toilet, I can sanctify that activity by viewing it as a gift to my wife, as an expression of love and a contribution to our shared life. I can also view cleaning the toilet as an act of service that flows out of my religious convictions, as an expression of the human being I want to become. When we sanctify a goal and activity, like cleaning the toilet, we expand the territory of the sacred in our everyday lives. Small, routine, and mundane activities become imbued with purpose and significance. We re-enchant our lives through the sanctification of goals.

Of course, some goals are more easily sanctified than others. Some goals, like intentional periods of prayer, are inherently sacred. Other goals are much less so. To be honest, cleaning my bathroom doesn't feel very enchanted to me. It feels like a chore and a bother. The same goes for many of the tedious and repetitious activities that fill up work and domestic life. Life can make you feel like Sisyphus rolling a rock up a hill over and over again. Yet it is precisely here where hope can become a discipline and a practice. We can practice resurrection through the intentional sanctification of daily life goals, connecting them to transcendent sources of meaning and value. We can *practice* story, purpose, and worth. Hope can become a habit.

A lovely illustration of this comes from the prayer book *Every Moment Holy* by Douglas Kaine McKelvey and

Ned Bustard. A tour through the table of contents captures the aspirations of the title as we find prayers and liturgies like these: "For Laundering," "Before Taking the Stage," "For the Changing of Diapers," "For Fiction Writers," "For Gardening," "For the Ritual of Morning Coffee," and "For Feasting with Friends." Every moment of life can become sanctified. And for the hope-sick, there are also prayers for difficult moments and seasons: "For a Sick Day," "For a Meal Eaten Alone," "For Those Flooded by Too Much Information," and "For Those Who Covet the Latest Technology." The second volume of *Every Moment Holy* is especially devoted to death, loss, and grief.

Regarding the sanctification and enchantment of routine, daily tasks, I love the prayer "For Domestic Days" from *Every Moment Holy*. A part of it reads:

Many are the things that must be daily done.
Meet me therefore, O Lord,
in the doing of the small, repetitive tasks,

In the cleaning and ordering and
maintenance and stewardship of things—
of dishes, of floors, of carpets
and toilets and tubs . . .

[S]o that in those ordered spaces
bright things might flourish. . . .

As I steward the small, daily tasks,
may I remember these good ends,
and so discover in my labors
the promise of the eternal hopes
that underlie them.

This is how we practice resurrection in a hope-sick world. Notice how the prayer re-enchants mundane life by leaning into a teleological imagination: small, daily tasks participate in "good ends" because our labors are not Sisyphean but share in "the promise of the eternal hopes that underlie them." Story, purpose, and worth become habits of the heart.

Crucially, this practice of hope doesn't lull or console us into passivity or complacency. Quite the opposite! Practicing hope is a *motivational* force in our lives, activating and sustaining fidelity to daily moral exertion. Practicing resurrection isn't wishful thinking. Practicing resurrection is, rather, commitment and continual re-commitment to the demands of the day, along with sustaining this effort across the lifespan.

In our modern, scientific, technological, secular, and post-Christian age, it might seem wildly naïve to say that heaven still matters. What could be more irrelevant and ridiculous in our disenchanted age than talk of pearly gates and streets of gold in a world facing environmental devastation, war, and rapacious greed? But I'll dare to say it: heaven still matters.

I don't mean, of course, heaven as an escapist, consoling illusion. I do wonder if Karl Marx, were he alive today, would want to revise his famous opinion that religion was the "opiate of the masses." Were Marx able to survey the vast array of narcoticizing products produced by capitalism—from cheap beer to social media to online porn to Netflix—I think he would stop blaming heaven for our lack of alarm as the world burns. To say nothing about how Marx's own materialistic vision of "progress" played out in Russia with the Gulag and Joseph Stalin murdering nine million people. Heaven, it turns out, is the least of Marx's problems.

Heaven matters because hope matters. Without teleology—without story, purpose, and worth—life becomes disenchanted, and we succumb either to despair or to the anesthetizing powers of consumer culture. But we are not defenseless. We are not Sisyphus, condemned to live, in the words of Henry David Thoreau, "lives of quiet desperation." We can practice resurrection. Every moment is holy. Sanctify the day.

Go live your beautiful life.

PART 3

ENCHANTED CHRISTIANITIES

8

LITURGICAL ENCHANTMENTS

I vividly remember my first Easter without liturgy. It surprised me how much I missed it.

You'll recall how in the sixth grade, as a dogmatic Protestant kid, I had started attending a Catholic school and how I had unwittingly participated in my first Ash Wednesday service. The horror!

We went to many mass services at Blessed Sacrament. After middle school, I attended Mercyhurst Prep, a Catholic high school. My years attending Catholic schools were regulated by the liturgical calendar, the feasts, holy days, and seasons of the church. While I suffered no more liturgical mishaps after my first Ash Wednesday service, most of this observance was lost on me. Most, that is, except for the Stations of the Cross.

We celebrated the Stations of the Cross on the Fridays of Lent. We'd begin with the first station—Jesus is condemned to death—and follow Jesus along the Via Dolorosa, his journey toward the cross. Stopping at each station, we'd pause to reflect and pray, soaking in Jesus's pain and suffering. In the end, we'd reach the fourteenth and final station—Jesus is laid in the tomb. And there the service concluded. No happy ending for this gathering. Every Friday, we'd end in darkness and sadness.

As a Protestant, nothing in my experience had prepared me for the Stations of the Cross. I'd never been to a church service that demanded I sit in sadness and lament for so long, and not just in a single service, but repeatedly, across many weeks. The Stations of the Cross had a profound and shattering impact upon me. Those days of sorrow with Jesus became etched upon my heart. Such is the power of liturgy. While my young Protestant mind raised all sorts of objections about Catholic observance during these years, with every passing Lent, the Stations of the Cross was shaping my heart.

I knew I had been permanently changed in my first year in college. I didn't attend a Catholic university. So for the first time since the sixth grade, I was completely free from the rhythms of the liturgical calendar, 100 percent back in a Protestant world. I didn't notice missing Advent. But things were different during the spring semester. One Sunday, someone mentioned that it was Easter. I was surprised, as I hadn't been paying attention to the calendar. This was before smartphones and social media, so it was easy for a busy college kid to lose track of

Easter. When I found out what day it was, I panicked. I remember the thought that flashed through my mind: "It can't be Easter. I'm not ready!"

That was the moment I realized just how Catholic I'd become. I didn't feel ready for Easter because I'd missed celebrating the Stations of the Cross during Lent. It felt off, Easter hitting me out of the blue, without a season of preparation and reflection. Easter wouldn't be Easter without Lent.

That feeling of unpreparedness during my first Easter without liturgy was a shock and a revelation to me. I never expected to miss liturgy and was stunned to find how much liturgy had affected and shaped me. That experience changed the way I viewed my years sitting bored and skeptical in Catholic Mass. I now realized that something more had been going on. And while I have remained a Protestant, a love and appreciation of liturgy began to grow in me—and not just liturgy, but the entire Catholic approach to spiritual formation, all the candles, incense, rosaries, stained glass, statues, and holy water. It wasn't just a feeling of nostalgia as a first-semester college student. In my adulthood, the enchantments of Catholicism would help save my Protestant faith.

Leaning on my training in psychology, I've described how we can re-enchant our faith in this skeptical age.

We can pay closer attention to the "strange sights," the many ways God speaks to us, every day, through religious experiences. We can pray prayers of Thanks, Help, and Wow to recover a sacramental ontology, where God is everywhere present in our one-story universe. And we can make the outward turns of hope, joy, gratitude, and mattering to receive the grace that comes to us as a gift.

But these aren't the only ways to enchant our faith. Christianity is full of enchanted traditions. I want us to survey four of these traditions: the liturgical, the contemplative, the charismatic, and the Celtic. There's no need to reinvent the wheel when it comes to enchantment. We're not starting from scratch. The history of Christianity provides us with many teachers. Enchantment can happen by recovering and reconnecting with some ancient Christian traditions. We can walk in the footsteps of the enchanted Christianities.

There's a saying among Catholics: "Matter matters."

One of the key insights of the Catholic liturgical tradition is that grace comes to us through the material world. The Spirit comes to us in the physical. The supernatural manifests itself in stuff. Matter matters.

Because matter matters, Catholic spirituality emphasizes our material, sensory reality. Physical objects are infused with a supernatural quality. Water is holy. You pray with beads. Objects are blessed. You cross yourself in prayer. Incense fills the room. Icons and statues adorn the walls. Ashes are smudged on your forehead. Homes have shrines.

This materiality strikes many Protestants as magical and superstitious, even pagan. Religious medals hanging from car mirrors can look a lot like magical talismans, and prayers of help to a saint can sound a lot like spells. It is true that Catholic spirituality has tipped into the magical and superstitious in various parts of the world as it fused and merged with indigenous, pagan spiritualities. But there is also wisdom here, especially for our skeptical age. The Protestant temptation to draw a hard line between the spiritual and the material relegates the spiritual to the invisible and unseen. This strict separation facilitates disenchantment as the visible, material world comes to be viewed as "real" and the unseen, spiritual world as "unreal." That's the temptation when we start making hard distinctions between the spiritual and the material.

This temptation is resisted in Catholicism, where matter matters. God approaches us through material reality, and we approach God through material reality. Spiritual and material are fused tightly together. The two cannot be separated. In this way, the Catholic imagination cultivates and preserves a sacramental ontology, where the spiritual is "everywhere present" and visible in the material world.

The material enchantments from Catholic and other liturgical traditions can help us push back against the forces of disenchantment. We can cultivate enchantment by curating our material surroundings and use material objects as aids in focusing our spiritual attention.

When matter matters, beauty matters. Aesthetics is one of the primary ways God speaks to us and tugs at our hearts. Beauty, natural or cultivated, prompts feelings of wonder, awe, and transcendence. Beautiful spaces are sacred spaces. Who hasn't experienced enchantment standing in a forest, strolling through a flower garden, beholding a cathedral, listening to a symphony, or witnessing a work of art? As C. S. Lewis observed, "We do not want merely to *see* beauty, though, God knows, even that is bounty enough. We want something else which can hardly be put into words—to be united with the beauty we see, to pass into it, to receive it into ourselves, to bathe in it, to become a part of it." Beauty is a tool for enchantment because beauty helps us recover our sacramental wonder.

Beyond beauty and aesthetics, we can fill our spaces with material reminders of spiritual realities. In the Catholic tradition, these are called sacramentals, material objects that draw our attention to God and excite spiritual devotion. Liturgical traditions are filled with sacramentals: icons, statues, artwork, crosses, candles, incense, altars, holy cards, crucifixes, scapulars, stained glass, prayer beads, art, jewelry, and medals. Sacramentals can be used to enchant your home and other personal spaces. My office is filled with icons, crucifixes, candles, and statues of saints who inspire me. A prayer kneeler is in a corner. I've enchanted my space. I can't go to work without being reminded of spiritual realities. The material objects filling both my home and office capture and direct my attention. In this skeptical world, it's easy for me to forget about God without physical, material reminders. So take a look at the spaces you inhabit. Your home, car, office. Look at what you wear around your neck, wrists, and fingers. Do you see material reminders of spiritual realities? If not, take some steps to enchant your world.

Beyond the material enchantments of beauty and the use of sacramentals helping us enchant *space*, liturgical traditions also help us enchant *time*. As we've described, time has become disenchanted in our skeptical age, stripped of its sacred character. My experience of the Stations of the Cross during Lent was my first exposure to enchanted time. Leaning into the liturgical calendar can help us re-enchant our days.

In my own faith journey, when my faith was at its lowest ebb, weakened by the battering waves of doubt and disenchantment, embracing the holy seasons of the church played a critical role in helping me hold on. I began to educate myself about the distinctions between Advent, a season of longing, and Christmas, a season of celebration. Two very different experiences! I learned that Christmas isn't a single-day celebration but an entire season lasting twelve whole days. I knew of the song "The Twelve Days of Christmas," but I never connected "a partridge in a pear tree" or "twelve lords a-leaping" with Christmastide, the liturgical season that begins at Vespers (evening prayers) on Christmas Eve and lasts until the Twelfth Night, January 5, the eve of the feast of the Epiphany (the celebration of the Wise Men visiting the Christ child). These discoveries helped me realize how my celebration of Christmas had been co-opted by the disenchanting forces of consumerism. For most of us, Christmas lasts not even a whole day. Once the presents are opened on Christmas morning, the season is pretty much over. Christmas is finished by lunchtime on the twenty-fifth as our thoughts turn to picking up all the wrapping paper and putting up the tree and decorations. It's unthinkable that we'd leave our trees, decorations, and Christmas greenery up for the full twelve days of Christmas, all the way to January 5. After lunch on Christmas, the world moves on, and so do we.

I began to re-enchant my life and faith by becoming more intentional in celebrating these holy seasons. I've learned to observe Advent as a season unto itself, and the

Christmas tree stays up all the way to January 5. Beyond Advent and Christmas, there is Lent and Easter. The Stations of the Cross are back in my life, along with all the other holy days and celebrations.

To be honest, if I can make a sad confession, I've become a bit of a liturgical snob about all of this. I've been known to express displeasure when "Joy to the World" is sung during Advent. ("Joy to the World" is a Christmas carol, a song of rejoicing and celebration. Advent hymns, by contrast, center themes of waiting, longing, and exile.) I work to temper this attitude in myself. My passion for the liturgical calendar is simply an expression of thankfulness. All my time and effort learning about, celebrating, and investing in the liturgical seasons recalibrated my attention and slowly re-enchanted my life. What time is it? I write this sentence on the Fourth Sunday of Advent. I know *exactly* what time it is. I'm not measuring my time with disenchanted clocks, with my vacation time from work or "national holidays" set in Washington. I number and celebrate my days with enchanted, sacred time.

The liturgical traditions show us how to push against disenchantment by paying attention to space and time. Nurture enchantment by attending to aesthetics and the use of sacramentals. Fill your spaces with material reminders of spiritual realities; cultivate your physical world like you'd cultivate a garden. Train your attention the same way you'd train your body. Beyond space, enchant time as well. Usher your heart and mind through sacred seasons and holy days. Wait during Advent. Celebrate during Christmas, all twelve days of it! Fast during Lent and party during Easter. Let God show you what time it is.

Face down this skeptical age by embracing the wisdom of the liturgical traditions. Matter matters. So light your candles. Hang your icons. Grab your prayer beads. Kneel in prayer. Linger with beauty. Deck your halls. And hallow your days.

9

CONTEMPLATIVE ENCHANTMENTS

Eighteen-year-old Nicholas gazed thoughtfully at the tree. It was winter, so the tree stood lifeless and bare, a black spider web of branches against the sky. A depressing sight in the bleak midwinter.

As Nicholas pondered the tree, a vision of spring came into his mind, the deadness of the tree giving way to life. He saw green buds bursting forth, leaves filling out the tree in an explosion of green, swaying joyfully in the sunlight. And then the fruit! Ripe, heavy, and sweet. Standing there in the cold, Nicholas could almost taste it.

This vision of spring, in that cold winter landscape, made Nicholas think of God. In the vision of the budding tree, Nicholas saw God's providential care, goodness, and love. God brings life out of death. Springtime out of snow.

The vision of spring became a conversion. At that moment, the love of God seized Nicholas's heart, filling it with joy. A joy Nicholas carried with him to the end of his days.

Nicholas's conversion occurred sometime around the year 1628 in France. Soon after, due to his extreme poverty, Nicholas signed up as a soldier in the Thirty Years' War. During the war, Nicholas suffered an injury that crippled him and would be a source of chronic pain for the rest of his life. The horrors of the war scarred Nicholas psychologically as well. As he convalesced, he found solace in God, revisiting the love he experienced in his vision of the tree. After he recovered, Nicholas worked briefly as a servant but eventually joined a Carmelite monastery at the age of twenty-six. In the monastery, Nicholas worked as a lay-brother in the kitchen, cooking for the community. Later, Nicholas would work in the sandal repair shop, and he continued to lend a hand in the kitchen when they needed help.

Called Brother Lawrence by the monks, Nicholas's steady demeanor of joy and peace while working the kitchen and sandal shop so affected the brothers and visitors of the monastery that he began to be sought out for spiritual guidance and direction. Wanting to capture the source of Nicholas's spiritual vitality and equanimity, Father Joseph de Beaufort interviewed Nicholas and collected some of his letters. In these conversations, Nicholas revealed his secret. For Nicholas, God was everywhere present. God was right there, in the hot kitchen and in the scrubbing of the pots. Our spiritual life consists, shared Nicholas, in making ourselves aware of God's presence, carrying on a constant conversation with God and doing everything, from slicing potatoes to mopping the floor, for the love of God. And when our thoughts stray, as they will, we bring our attention back toward God. The spiritual life, exhorted Nicholas, doesn't consist of doing or adding religious activities to our lives, sprinkling a bit of religious tinsel onto our workweeks. The religious life consists of doing exactly what you are already doing—your daily work and domestic routine, from the work commute to washing laundry to balancing the Excel spreadsheet—with an awareness of God's presence and love. Work and prayer are not two distinct activities. "The time of business," Nicholas said, "does not with me differ from the time of prayer. In the noise and clutter of my kitchen, while several persons are at the same time calling for different things, I possess God in as great tranquility as if I were upon my knees at the Blessed Supper." In this daily effort of disciplined attention, in the boring and busy parts of our day, we practice the presence of God. Through this practice, we slowly acquire a habitual, moment-by-moment awareness of God's presence. We can wash the dishes, as Nicholas did, and feel God everywhere present, our hearts full of peace and joy.

Joseph de Beaufort's collection of letters and interviews with Brother Lawrence was eventually published as *The Practice of the Presence of God*, a book that would become one of the most beloved works in the Christian contemplative tradition. If re-enchantment is fundamentally a practice of attention, attuning ourselves to the "strange sights," then we find in Brother Lawrence a wise teacher. *The Practice of the Presence of God*—and the whole of the Christian contemplative tradition—provides us with tools for pushing back against the forces of disenchantment. For at its heart, the contemplative tradition emphasizes attention and awareness. This is exactly what we need if disenchantment is fundamentally a form of "attention blindness," failing to see the dancing gorilla right in front of us. But awareness of God's presence doesn't emerge out of thin air. Awareness is effortful and practiced. Consequently, the contemplative tradition also points us toward spiritual disciplines. As Brother Lawrence shows us, we *practice* the presence of God. Both enchantment and disenchantment are *habits*, habits of attention or inattention, awareness or obliviousness.

As a companion of the liturgical enchantments where "matter matters," the contemplative tradition in Christianity is a deep and rich resource for re-enchantment—and a very practical resource, at that. By focusing on our awareness of God and involving us in spiritual disciplines, the contemplative tradition habituates us back toward enchantment in this skeptical age. We come to see the "strange sights" by practicing the presence of God.

St. Ignatius helped Jana and me as parents. When our two sons were little, Jana and I used to have them reflect upon their day by sharing with us "roses and thorns." A "rose" was a happy, joyful part of the day. A "thorn" was a sad or difficult part of the day. As Brenden and Aidan shared the "roses and thorns" of the day, Jana and I could help them discern God's presence in their lives. By drawing attention to the movement of their hearts, where they were sad and anxious and where they were peaceful and happy, our prayers with the boys were less about asking God for things than cultivating an *awareness* of God.

"Roses and thorns" is an example of the Ignatian practice of examen. Ignatius of Loyola (1491–1556) was the founder of the Jesuits. Beyond founding the Jesuits, St. Ignatius is famous for being the author of the *Spiritual Exercises*, a manual for prayer, discernment, and spiritual direction. Similar to Brother Lawrence's *The Practice of the Presence of God*, Ignatius's *Spiritual Exercises* is considered to be one of the crown jewels of the contemplative tradition, a how-to handbook for contemplation. As originally envisioned by Ignatius, the spiritual exercises involve a four-week retreat with a spiritual director, what Jesuits call "the long retreat." However, the "four weeks" of the exercises are meant to be flexible, four movements rather than literal weeks. Most laypeople spread the "four weeks" across many months. Ignatius builds in flexibility to create this "retreat in daily life," suggesting an hour of prayer each day under the guidance of a spiritual director. Today, the *Spiritual Exercises* is perhaps the most influential text in Christian spiritual formation and direction. If you seek spiritual direction, odds are you'll be doing something, at some point, suggested by St. Ignatius.

The point of the *Spiritual Exercises* is cultivating an attentiveness, awareness, openness, and receptivity toward God. This is exactly what we need in our disenchanted age, practical advice on how to turn our attention toward God. The practices of the *Spiritual Exercises* get us into the habit of assuming an eccentric posture where we look toward the eucatastrophe—help coming to us from the outside.

According to St. Ignatius, among all the exercises, meditations, and prayers he recommends in the *Spiritual Exercises*, by far the most important is the prayer of examen. If you were only able to pray one prayer a day, said St. Ignatius, make it the prayer of examen.

Like Jana and I did with Brenden and Aidan, in the prayer of examen, we survey and review our day, hour by hour, looking for "roses and thorns." In the Ignatian tradition, these roses and thorns are called consolations and desolations. Emotions are our key guide in this process. When during the day did you feel angry, irritated, stressed, impatient, anxious, agitated, tense, ashamed, defeated, sad, guilty, depressed, or worthless? These are the moments of desolation, the thorns. By contrast, when during your day did you feel peaceful, joyful, relaxed, happy, and whole? These are the roses, the moments of consolation.

Beyond feelings, we also attend to our words and actions throughout the day. When today did I speak rashly, harshly, or thoughtlessly? Did I gossip or cut others down? Did my words bring comfort, support, praise, grace, or encouragement? Where did I extend kindness and gentleness? When did I act selfishly, rudely, aggressively, or meanly?

The point of this emotional, verbal, and behavioral inventory is to discern the movement of God in my day, minute by minute, hour by hour. The goal of examen isn't to tally up your sins and failures from the day. The focus of examen is *discernment*. Where in my day am I being drawn toward God? And when am I being pulled away? When you're disciplined in praying the prayer of examen, you'll begin to note patterns in your life. You'll notice how the roses and thorns tend to cluster around certain places, people, times, and activities. As you make these observations, you can begin to make adjustments, really leaning into and savoring the moments of consolation while becoming more intentional about addressing what triggers the moments of desolation.

Let me give you a small but significant illustration of this in my own life. I don't know about you, but I'm a pretty busy, distracted person. Consequently, I can be physically present with people but not emotionally or mentally present. For instance, I like to write in the morning over my morning coffee. But Jana also likes to visit with me in the mornings. So I listen to Jana, but not really. I half listen as I type. And sometimes I grow irritated. But other mornings, I shut my laptop and lean into the conversation, listening and asking questions. On these mornings, instead of irritation, I feel us growing closer together and happier.

I noticed all this about Jana and me through praying the prayer of examen. I noticed recurring thorns every morning, that when I kept my laptop open and half listened to Jana, I was irritated and impatient. But I also noticed roses, the happiness I felt when I shut my laptop to really participate in the conversation. Discerning this, I began to make it a habit to shut my laptop the second Jana joined me at the kitchen table to become fully present.

This is a small, domestic example, but it's an important one. Our lives are built out of small moments just like these. Moments and interactions with spouses, children, friends, coworkers, social media, and the strangers we stand behind in the checkout line at the store. Remember Tolkien's observation that fairy stories help us *recover* the world, especially the people we love. If you want to experience more enchantment in your life, more magical, mystical moments where the world shines like transfiguration, the Ignatian practice of examen is a huge help.

When I shut my laptop and turn my attention to Jana, I *recover* her. Morning coffee becomes an enchanted, sacred moment. And mornings with Jana is just the start. When I pay attention, I experience the magic in a million other little moments over the course of my day. But I have to pay attention. Just like Moses and the burning bush, we must turn aside to behold the vision. Examen is this turning aside. You train yourself to enchant the day.

One of my favorite examples of how attention enchants our lives is from the late author David Foster Wallace in his famous commencement address "This Is Water," delivered to the graduates of Kenyon College. In his talk, Wallace describes the tedium and irritations we face in modern life, the "parts of adult American life that nobody talks about in commencement speeches," the parts of our day that involve "boredom, routine, and petty frustration." Wallace observes that these troubles are caused by our failures of attention: "It is extremely difficult to stay alert and attentive, instead of getting hypnotized by the constant monologue inside your own head." To illustrate this, Wallace has us imagine standing in a long checkout line at the store after a brutal, exhausting day at work. We know, as Wallace comments, that our days are full of these "dreary, annoying, seemingly meaningless routines." But it's here, says Wallace, in the middle of our exhaustion and irritation, where the "work of choosing" comes into play, choosing "how to pay attention." Because if we don't pay attention, our emotional default will be to gaze upon these strangers with loathing and anger. As Wallace describes it, in "my hungriness and my fatigue and my desire to just get home . . . it's going to seem, for all the world, like everybody else is just *in my way.* . . . I've worked really hard all day and I'm starved and tired and I can't even get home to eat and unwind because of all these stupid goddamn *people.*" I'm sure you can sympathize; life is full of these moments. And yet, even here, enchantment can happen. *If we pay attention.* As Wallace continues,

[But rather than looking at my situation this way,] I can choose to force myself to consider the likelihood that everyone else in the supermarket's checkout line is just as bored and frustrated as I am, and that some of these people actually have much harder, more tedious or painful lives than I do. . . .

[I]t's hard. It takes will and effort. . . . But if you really learn how to pay attention . . . [i]t will actually be within your power to experience a crowded, hot, slow, consumer-hell-type situation as not only meaningful, but sacred, on fire with the same force that lit the stars: compassion, love, the subsurface unity of all things.

That's the "strange sight." This is Thomas Merton standing at Fourth and Walnut realizing he loved total strangers. This is seeing the dancing gorilla, right there in that long line at the supermarket. And it happens because of *attention*—disciplined, intentional, effortful attention. As Wallace concludes, attention enchants the world, because it's through attention that we "get to decide what to worship."

Disciplines like the Ignatian prayer of examen or Brother Laurence's practicing the presence of God get us to this crossroads, this moment of choice. In surveying our thorns and roses, we can plan and prepare to practice the presence of God in the desolations of the day. Maybe that desolation is your impatience with being interrupted over morning coffee, or maybe it's standing in a long line at the store. Regardless, roses can bloom where before only thorns were found. With your attention, you get to decide in those moments what to worship. You can make the choice to turn aside to behold the "strange sight," to see the world burn with the "force that lit the stars: compassion, love, the subsurface unity of all things."

Everywhere I go, I carry with me a *chotki*, an Orthodox prayer rope. In the Eastern Orthodox tradition, knotted prayer ropes are used to count prayers rather than stringed beads, like the rosary in the Catholic tradition. The chotki knot is quite a complicated knot to tie (seriously, watch a YouTube tutorial to see for yourself).

Usually made out of wool, common Orthodox prayer ropes have 33 (each knot for a year of Christ's life), 100, or 150 knots. Orthodox monastics have ropes with up to 300 or 500 knots.

In the Orthodox tradition, the knots on the prayer rope are used to count repetitions of the Jesus Prayer, one of the most ancient and venerated prayers from the contemplative Christian tradition: "Lord Jesus Christ, Son of God, have mercy on me, a sinner." Using the prayer rope, you say the Jesus prayer over and over again as you move your fingers from knot to knot. In the middle of my day, walking the dog or standing in that hellishly long line at the supermarket, I'll pull out my prayer rope and begin praying through the knots. If I'm having trouble focusing my attention, struggling to see the "force that lit the stars," physically holding my prayer rope and having some structured words to say, like the Jesus Prayer, is very helpful.

These prayer aids, like beads or knotted ropes, along with structured prayers, like the Jesus Prayer, are other resources that come to us from the contemplative Christian tradition. Sometimes it's hard to "pay attention" without a physical object to hold and to guide or focus us. Feeling prayer beads in my pocket or seeing the prayer rope on my wrist can trigger and recall my attention back to practicing the presence of God. Again, matter matters! Likewise, sometimes words are hard when it comes to prayer. So having something structured to say like the Jesus Prayer or the Lord's Prayer can help.

The world of prayer is vast, and I cannot do it justice. Let me encourage you to explore books like Richard Foster's *Prayer: Finding the Heart's True Home* or Martin Laird's *Into the Silent Land: A Guide to the Christian Practice of Contemplation.* In the contemplative tradition, prayers like the Jesus Prayer are sometimes called "breath prayers" or "arrow prayers," a prayer that is just a single sentence or word. Sometimes when I'm having hostile thoughts toward others, I'll pull out my prayer rope and say the word *mercy* over and over, knot after knot. Other times, when stressed or anxious, I'll pray the word *peace.* These short sentences or single words are prayerful "arrows" we shoot toward heaven, which can be coupled with meditative breathing. Take in a breath with the words "Lord Jesus Christ, Son of God." Exhale with "Have mercy on me, a sinner." Find words and Scriptures to craft prayers that bless you, and practice these prayers until the words become automatic and habitual, like breath itself.

Beyond breath prayers, I've mentioned how I use the Liturgy of the Hours for structured prayers offered during fixed hours of the day. Few nonmonastics pray all the hours, but one can create a prayer routine by selecting some of the hours or specific times to pray regularly during the day. There are even smartphone prayer apps that can help. As I shared, my practice has been to pray in the morning and evening each day using the structured prayers from either *The Book of Common Prayer* (from the Anglican/Episcopalian tradition) or *The Divine Office* (from the Catholic tradition). These aren't your only options. Many of my friends have found Phyllis Tickle's three-volume *The Divine Hours* very helpful in establishing a fixed-hour prayer routine. These structured prayers have been a lifeline for me when I struggled with prayer during seasons of doubt and disenchantment. When I had no words, the words of the Psalms and the church carried me, enchanting my life when God seemed silent and distant.

Beyond prayer, these habits and routines embrace all the practices described as "spiritual disciplines": practices of fasting, Sabbath, Scripture reading, simplicity, and silence. As with prayer, the resources available to explore here are enormous. Pick up Richard Foster's classic *The Celebration of Discipline* or dip into Adele Calhoun's exhaustive *Spiritual Disciplines Handbook*. And you don't have to go on this journey alone. Seek out a spiritual director, attend a contemplative retreat, or ask a small group of friends to accompany you in practicing a form of prayer or discipline. Again, enchantment is all about attention, and the contemplative tradition gives us so many resources to shape, habit, direct, and discipline our hearts and minds.

But let's not mistake the means for the end. Practicing the presence of God, the Ignatian practice of examen, the Jesus Prayer, the fixed-hour prayer, and the spiritual disciplines are tools of *contemplation*, time-tested methods that bring us face-to-face with the mystery of God. Prayer practices and spiritual disciplines aren't pietistic activities we do in order to be "good Christians." They are tools to facilitate an encounter with God.

This encounter with God, the contemplative tradition teaches us, transcends rational description. Prayer ushers us into the mystery of God, that place where words fail us. We've talked about this, how religious experiences have an ineffable, unsayable, and indescribable quality. Christianity can be a very verbal and intellectual faith. This is a good thing, but it has its temptations. Our experience with God tends to lose its relational character, where enchantment thrives, when it becomes overly intellectualized. Instead of an *encounter* with God, we have *ideas* about God. Too many words about God—too much talking, reading, and listening about God—can disenchant our faith. We trade a *relationship* with God for *knowledge* about God. But life with God isn't a test; it's a love affair.

Prayer is that place where we become disciplined in setting words and ideas aside in the face of the mystery. Thomas Merton describes contemplation as "spiritual wonder" and "spontaneous awe at the sacredness of life." Contemplation, says Merton, is "a vivid realization of the fact that life and being in us proceed from an invisible, transcendent and infinitely abundant Source.

Contemplation is, above all, awareness of the reality of that Source." And again, this awareness goes beyond ideas and words. "Contemplation," says Merton, "is always beyond our own knowledge, beyond our own light, beyond system, beyond explanations, beyond discourse, beyond dialogue, beyond your own self." This nonverbal, contemplative awareness is the path toward enchantment. Through contemplation, we experience "a vivid awareness of infinite Being at the roots of our own contingent reality as received, as a present of God, as a free gift of love." This is the eucatastrophe, receiving and experiencing our lives as a free gift of love from the Source of our gratitude, hope, joy, and mattering. The mystics describe this awareness of God's loving Presence as a form of awakening and enlightenment. Suddenly, the world shines like transfiguration, and the Love of God becomes everywhere present. This is the recovery of the world we find in fairy stories, regaining our sacramental imagination. "For it is God's love," declares Merton,

that warms me in the sun and God's love that sends the cold rain. It's is God's love that feeds me in the bread I eat and God that feeds me by hunger and fasting. It is the love of God that sends the winter days when I am cold and sick, and the hot summer when I labor and my clothes are full of sweat. . . . [I]t is God Who breathes on

me with light winds off the river and the breezes
out of the wood. His love spreads the shade of
the sycamore over my head. . . . It is God's love
that speaks to me in the birds and streams.

These are the gifts of the contemplative tradition, calling us to awareness and mystery. Enroll yourself in this school of prayer. Invest in spiritual wonder. Seeds of awareness, as signs of God's love, drift on the air like dandelion tufts.

10

CHARISMATIC ENCHANTMENTS

About seven years ago, my faith was at a very low ebb. Waves of doubt had worn my faith down to the point where it was almost nonexistent.

After reading a lot of books, I eventually convinced myself that I couldn't think or read myself out of this jam. In fact, I came to the conclusion that thinking and reading were a huge part of my problem. I had turned God into an intellectual puzzle I had to solve. The goal of faith became developing deep and sophisticated theological opinions on an array of issues, controversies, and questions. The problem of evil and suffering. The violence we find in the Old Testament. The nature of the atonement. How to make science jibe with the Bible. The moral witness of the apostle Paul on the issues of gender roles and slavery. The nature of God's judgment and hell.

The guiding principle of my faith during this season was that a vibrant and healthy spiritual life involved
tenaciously pursuing all these questions and getting
some answers. Better answers and a better way of reading the Bible were the goals. So for decades, my spiritual
life consisted of reading and thinking hard about God
and Scripture. Eventually, though, and perhaps ironi-
cally, this pursuit slowly eroded my faith. I was, to put it
plainly, too much in my head. The wheels wouldn't stop
spinning. I couldn't pray because prayer was one of the
things I had questions about. I couldn't worship, because
I had too many theological disagreements with the lyrics
of the songs we were singing. I walked away from sermon
after sermon with long lists of questions and objections.
Over time, I'd cut myself off from God, trapping myself in
a prison of words and ideas. I was lost in a maze of questions and doubts.

Eventually it dawned upon me that this intellectual
quest was making me spiritually sick. God wasn't a Rubik's
Cube to solve but a living reality to encounter. But it had
been so long since I'd prayed, truly prayed, that I found
I couldn't anymore. *The Book of Common Prayer* and *The
Divine Office* came to my aid here, gifting me words when
I had none of my own. I also decided I needed a change
of location. I'm a college professor, and the spiritual climate of university life isn't always the healthiest, even on
a Christian campus like my own. University professors,
given their occupation of scholarly inquiry and debate,

can tend toward the critical, skeptical, cynical, and ironic. As a professor, this was precisely my own problem, so I needed to get to a place that didn't reinforce those tendencies within me. That's how I found myself sitting in the back pew of Freedom Fellowship.

Freedom is a small mission church in a poor part of our town, planted by my home congregation. Every Wednesday at Freedom, we serve a meal for our neighbors, and a praise service follows. Our friends and neighbors at Freedom are often poor or homeless. Many are struggling with addiction. We've got friends who are on parole. Socially and economically, Freedom was a million miles away from my college campus. It seemed the very best place to go looking for God.

What I found at Freedom threw me for a loop. Freedom is a very charismatic congregation, and I grew up in a very staid, reserved, nonexpressive, and nonemotional faith tradition. You kept your butts in the pew and hands at your side. Things couldn't have been more different at Freedom. At Freedom, hands are raised during worship. People wave prayer flags. Worshippers dance. Once at Freedom, a sort of Holy Ghost conga line broke out during worship. Someone started dancing around the auditorium, and everyone joined in, a whole line of worshippers dancing and praising God, circling the space. This happened early in my time at Freedom, so I sat inhibited and awkward in my seat, electing to give supportive high fives as the conga line passed me. But slowly, over time, the charismatic worship of Freedom began to work on my heart. The praise experience at Freedom re-enchanted my faith by reconnecting my mind with both my body and heart. I don't wave the flags, and I'm still not a big hand raiser. But my heart sings at Freedom, and for the first time in my life, I lift my hands in worship. The charismatics and their conga lines rescued my faith.

The charismatic and pentecostal traditions may be the most enchanted streams of Christianity. I'm going to use small-*c* and small-*p* spellings of *charismatic* and *pentecostal* to describe a type of spirituality that transcends and cuts across denominational lines. As I'm using the words, you can be a charismatic Catholic, Methodist, or Baptist. By *charismatic* or *pentecostal*, I mean a strongly felt experience of the Holy Spirit's presence and activity in our lives, often through "signs and wonders." In response to God's presence and activity, charismatic and pentecostal worship is characterized by full-bodied, energetic, and emotional praise, thanksgiving, and testimony. This is the spirituality of Freedom Fellowship. God is alive and powerfully at work in our lives, and our response to God's gifts is an outpouring of praise, those Holy Ghost conga lines. That I found a charismatic experience at Freedom, where many of our friends are poor and homeless, keeps to a global pattern. Charismatic spirituality flourishes among the poor and the oppressed in America and across the world. In the West, the educated and affluent struggle mightily with disenchantment and skepticism. Western elites are crippled by their religious doubts. Just as I was before I started attending Freedom. But enchantment thrives on the margins of society.

To be sure, there are issues we need to navigate here. I promise before you reach the last page that we'll talk about issues of spiritual discernment. Not everything we find in charismatic or pentecostal churches and movements is healthy. Many have been hurt by charismatic spirituality, and there are a variety of problematic theologies, like the Prosperity Gospel, that thrive in this sector of the Christian landscape. In addition, for the doubting and skeptical, the charismatic and pentecostal experience might be a bit *too* enchanted, too much of a leap of faith. From faith healings, to speaking in tongues, to hearing a "word from the Lord," to miracle stories, to deliverance/exorcism ministries, the charismatic world can be a step too far for the skeptical, incredulous, questioning Christian. A Holy Ghost conga line could make you run for the exit signs. I was a fish out of water when I first attended Freedom. Charismatic spirituality has its temptations, excesses, and blind spots. But so does the detached, critical, and skeptical faith of disenchanted privileged elites. And in my experience, the temptations of disenchantment are far more dangerous. Let's remember what Chris Arnade discovered about faith on the streets of back-row

America. I find the excesses of charismatic theology easily addressable, a simple matter of inserting some critical nuance and attending to the lament and brokenness of life. Disenchantment, by contrast, is a faith killer.

So while there are some things to monitor and be concerned about in charismatic spaces, and the stories here are numerous, let's not throw the Holy Ghost out with the bathwater. Along with the liturgical and contemplative traditions, charismatic and pentecostal spiritualities have much to teach us about enchantment.

"Praise God! Hallelujah!"

I'm sitting at Freedom while a dear sister shares her testimony, a story of how God has been faithful, rescuing her from a broken home, sexual abuse, addiction, and homelessness. As the story unfolds, voices ring out expressing gratitude and praise. "Praise God! Hallelujah!"

Testimonies like this are a staple of charismatic spaces. When you give your testimony, you share your personal story about how God has saved you, leading you from darkness to light. At Freedom, given the difficult lives of our members, these stories are often harrowing and gut wrenching. Stories of abuse, trauma, violence, addiction, prison time, and homelessness. But weaving in and out of the pain is a ribbon of grace, God showing up in unlikely moments and people. A testimony is about how "God is good," even in the darkest moments, because God is always there, protecting and providing, keeping us sane and alive until we could reach this moment of wholeness, health, and community. Testimonies are stories of surprising grace.

Testimonies are also filled with miracle stories, stories of physical healing, money showing up just when you're about to get evicted, answered prayers, and chance encounters. Each miracle story is evidence of God's providential presence and care, received by the audience with exclamations of "Praise God!" and "Hallelujah!" At Freedom, miracles are *expected*. Miracles are not rare or exceptional; they are daily and routine. And why wouldn't they be? God is alive and at work.

Doubting, skeptical, and disenchanted Christians struggle mightily with miracles. Locked in their heads by chains of analytical reasoning, many disenchanted Christians attack miracle stories with a battery of questions. Every miracle story is fiercely interrogated as a "more rational" explanation is sought. Perhaps that chance encounter or the money in the mail wasn't God but a mere coincidence. Perhaps the doctors, rather than God, healed that person. We've all asked these sorts of questions and expressed these doubts when faced with stories we find too incredible or too neat and tidy to believe. Some of us, especially those of us who have been thoroughly disenchanted by the modern, scientific world, just can't stop raising these questions. We doubt *every* miracle story. We are downright *allergic* to enchantment. We are compulsive doubters and addictively skeptical.

I was like that when I first started attending Freedom. During our testimonies, instead of raising my hands in praise, I'd raise a question in my mind. But over time, the testimonies and praise of Freedom began to work on my heart. Cracks started forming in the wall of logic and rationality I had erected between myself and God.

What I learned at Freedom is that miracle stories are *a hermeneutics of gratitude*. In my early days at Freedom, whenever I heard a miracle story, the skeptical wheels of my brain would start to spin. Was that really God at work? Couldn't it have been a lucky coincidence? But in his book *Thinking in Tongues*, James Smith describes the heart of charismatic spirituality as standing in "a position of radical openness to God, and in particular, God doing something differently or new." This charismatic posture is a posture of *receptivity*. And over time, I began to realize that my brothers and sisters at Freedom were showing me, in their expressions of gratitude and praise, what a posture of receptivity looks like in day-to-day life. Yes, we could debate why that money showed up in the mail to pay the bill, but the fact remains, the money showed up. Help came. And we could debate why that person was healed. But the fact remains, a loved one was restored to health. Help came. Miracle stories, I came to understand, are *a practice of attention*, the charismatic habit of noticing how grace and rescue flow through every

moment of your life, even the smallest and most insignif-
icant. I used to scoff at stories of finding a parking spot
just when you needed it. But still, help came. Because of
that parking spot, you weren't late for your important
meeting. And you receive that small grace with gratitude.
Miracle stories are practices of dependence and thanksgiving, habits of prayers of Help followed by prayers of
Thanks. This is why I described miracle stories as herme-
neutical, as an *interpretive* activity. You can tell the story
of your life in any number of ways. For the skeptical and
disenchanted, your life is a story of chance and coincidence, rolls of the dice. You can be lucky in such a story,
but you can never be truly grateful, not really. Luck isn't
a gift. Chance isn't grace. My brothers and sisters at Freedom choose to tell their stories differently. They tell fairy
stories, stories of enchantment. They tell miracles stories.
Their stories are full of gratitude because their stories
are full of grace. God is at work everywhere. Help came.
"Praise God! Hallelujah!"

"You can't do that in here."

These words were spoken to me the first time I taught
the Beatitudes in the maximum-security prison where I
lead a Bible study. Our talk was running along smoothly
as we discussed the list of the blessed—"Blessed are those
who hunger and thirst for righteousness. Blessed are

the poor in spirit. Blessed are those who mourn." But I noticed a change in the men whenever we got to talking about "Blessed are the meek." The voices got quieter, the conversation lagged, and I detected a note of skepticism. "It doesn't look like you guys are buying this," I said to the class. There was an awkward silence in the room, and then someone said what was on everyone's mind: "You can't do that in here."

In a maximum-security prison, the men shared, meekness is taken for weakness. And you can't be perceived as weak in prison. Weakness is dangerous. Weakness will get you hurt. So while the men understood what Jesus was asking of them in the Sermon on the Mount, they felt that self-preservation demanded they reject this particular Beatitude. It was the safer, more prudent course. As the theologian Stanley Hauerwas said, "To be kind in a violent world is very dangerous." No one knows that better than the men in my Bible study.

The night I heard those words about the Sermon on the Mount—"You can't do that in here"—was the night I started believing in the devil.

James Smith points out that another feature of charismatic spirituality is how charismatic Christians are very aware of what some have called "spiritual warfare." Descriptions of spiritual warfare take their cue from Ephesians 6:11–12: "Put on the whole armor of God, so that you may be able to stand against the wiles of the devil. For our struggle is not against enemies of blood and flesh, but against the rulers, against the authorities, against the cosmic powers of this present darkness, against the spiritual forces of evil in the heavenly places." Spiritual warfare is the battle against "spiritual forces of evil in the heavenly places." Among charismatic Christians, this is a struggle between demonic and angelic forces, fought with prayer, Scripture, and using the name of Jesus to "bind the strong man" (Mark 3:23–27 KJV). Spiritual warfare takes place in an enchanted world, a world full of dark, unseen forces seeking to attack and undermine the Kingdom of God.

Like miracle stories, spiritual warfare is hard for the skeptical and disenchanted. Angels and demons seem to be relics of a superstitious past. Sure, people still believe in ghosts and guardian angels, but many people in our skeptical age think that stuff is silly. Start talking about demons at work and watch your lunch invitations evaporate. Science and technology have pushed these enchantments to the fringes.

That's how I saw things when I started leading the Bible study out at the prison. I was a passionate follower of Jesus, finding his love for the poor and oppressed a model for how I should live my life. Jesus was the GOAT of social justice warriors, the Greatest of All Time. Outside of this very narrow moral and political understanding of Christianity, I didn't have much time for the spookier, more enchanted aspects of the faith. Battling with "spiritual forces of evil in the heavenly places" wasn't on my radar screen.

All that changed with the words "You can't do that in here." When I heard those words, I came face-to-face with the dark force that makes kindness dangerous. The Kingdom of God was facing a headwind, swimming upstream against a fierce, relentless, countervailing current. This dark current is at work everywhere if you look for it, but it took a prison for me to finally see it clearly. Prison has this clarifying effect. The moral contrasts are starker and sharper, allowing those of us with weak spiritual vision to see more clearly. I started believing in the devil that night out at the prison because the force in the world opposing Jesus tooth and nail finally came into my view. That's what *Satan* means, after all; it means "adversary," that which "stands opposed" to you. Satan is that force in the world that makes kindness dangerous.

The enchanted world of Christianity isn't safe. If you've gotten the impression that enchantment is just rainbows and cotton candy, you've missed the point. Christian enchantment isn't spacey supernaturalism, emotional uplift, or credulous kookiness. There is a whole lot of that stuff going around, and I'm going to talk about it. But the point I want to emphasize here is that Christian enchantment is a struggle, a call to battle. One of the gifts of the charismatic tradition is how it helps us recover this vision, this call to "spiritual warfare."

By and large, disenchanted Christians have lost touch with this struggle. In a disenchanted world, the only actors left on the stage are human beings. This *moralizes* and *politicizes* our faith. We strive to be moral in how we treat each other and struggle to wrest control away from political opponents. What this vision misses, according to theologian Fleming Rutledge, is that in the biblical worldview, there's actually a "third power" involved in the drama. Beyond God and human beings, there's also Satan, the dark force at work in the world. Charismatic enchantment draws our attention to this "third power" in our lives.

I understand how skeptical Christians might struggle with how to envision this "third power." Let me suggest that we don't get too literal and simply pay attention to the world around us. When you pay attention, what you come to realize is that every inch of your life and every moment of your day is hotly contested territory. There is no neutral ground. We are always standing at a moral and spiritual crossroads. You're dealing with a fragile marriage. A troubled child. A nasty boss. An irritating coworker. An unfulfilling job. A triggering event. A lost election. A social media feed. A traumatic past. A growing addiction. A brutal work commute. A failed dream. A stack of bills. A life regret. A closet of shame. A mental illness. A lack of friends. A social snub. A forgiveness that hasn't been extended. A cancer diagnosis. A sin that hasn't been confessed. A pain that hasn't been healed. A grace that hasn't been accepted. A grudge that continues to be nurtured.

Shall I go on?

Life is a never-ending series of moral challenges
and choices. And you don't get a moment off. There is
no halftime or time-outs. Act or refuse to act, each deci-
sion determines your destiny, the moral arc of your life.
The darkness is always close at hand, and we fight it off,
hour by hour. The skeptical world doesn't get this, the
moral intensity and urgency of life, but the Bible sure
does. As it says in 1 Peter 5:8: "Discipline yourselves, keep
alert. Like a roaring lion your adversary the devil prowls
around, looking for someone to devour." We've all felt
it, the moist, hot breath of the predator on our neck as
we've stood alone the darkness. The Christian life isn't
just about moral self-improvement or getting your team
to win the next election. Our days are spent in the spiritual trenches, in the private dramas of our lives, where we
stand at the moral crossroads, over and over again, choosing to do the next right thing.

The charismatic enchantment of spiritual warfare
isn't spacey, naive, or kooky. If you're honest, you'll see
the truth: You're in a fight. Spiritual warfare is your life.
Which means we need help to come to us "from the outside." We need divine assistance, God's eucatastrophe.
Fighting in the trenches, we need to pray the prayer of
Help.

While the disenchanted and skeptical might wave
all this talk about the devil away as an outdated fiction,
I think enchantment has the truth on this score. I've felt
the hot breath of the predator on my neck. And I bet you

have as well. However you want to imagine it, there's a "third power" out there, relentlessly seeking to devour us. The darkness is always close at hand, one catastrophic choice away. So let's do what the charismatics do: let's pray for help and stay awake.

> The heart has its reasons which reason does not know. We feel it in a thousand things. . . .
>
> It is the heart which experiences God, and not the reason. This, then, is faith; God felt by the heart, not by reason.

These words were written by the famous mathematician and Christian mystic Blaise Pascal (1623–62). You'll recall Pascal as the guy who sewed a handwritten account of his encounter with God inside his coat. Pascal was a Catholic, but his words here perfectly capture another aspect of charismatic spirituality, the role of *emotions* in encountering and experiencing God.

Excessive rationality is an enemy of enchantment. As Pascal says, it is the *heart* that experiences God. When you live too much in your head, you cut yourself off from God. This isn't to say that you turn your brain off as a Christian, that enchantment requires becoming credulous and gullible. It is, rather, the simple truth that the heart *has its own reasons*, its own way of knowing and determining the truth. The great lie of our scientific, skeptical world is that science has become the sole arbiter and judge of "the truth." We've been deceived into thinking that if something isn't "scientific," it isn't "true." But a moment's reflection shows this is simply ridiculous. As Pascal notes, we see the evidence of this "in a thousand things." I don't know the love I have for Jana because of the scientific method. I don't verify the joy I experience looking at a West Texas sunset in a test tube or petri dish. I don't measure the beauty I experience before a great work of art. I don't make moral decisions by applying the laws of physics. And I can't find the story that gives my life purpose, value, meaning, and direction written in any equation penned by the late Stephen Hawking. I know we're all deeply grateful to science. I love air conditioning and antibiotics. But *the truest things in my life are feelings*, not facts.

This is why excessive rationality is so corrosive to faith. Rather than leading you toward the truth, excessive rationality cuts you off from the truth. Instead of being a human being, you're acting like a computer, all analysis and no feeling. You've amputated your heart. You don't calculate an equation to justify saying "I love you." You don't do an experiment before shedding a tear. But we insist on finding God in this half-human, robotic, calculating manner. At the end of the day, recovering enchantment is really very simple: embrace being a human being.

The heart has its reasons, and you feel it in a thousand things.

This is how Freedom Fellowship saved my faith, by reuniting it with my heart. Charismatic worship, with those Holy Ghost conga lines, is full-bodied and emotional. I didn't jump in immediately when I first started attending Freedom. But over time, the praise experience of Freedom thawed my heart and moved my body. When I first raised my hands in worship at Freedom—for the first time in my life—I embraced a truth that my intellect could never reveal. There are things your heart knows that your mind just doesn't.

This makes you wonder why men are more likely to be atheists than women. For example, James Smith makes the observation that sexism may be one of the reasons so many men are judgmental and dismissive of emotional praise music. Much of this emotionalism in praise and worship music has been dismissed as too "romantic" and even "erotic," sneered at as "Jesus is my boyfriend" music. But in this snobbery toward "mushy" emotional praise music, Smith detects a hint of chauvinism:

> [A focus on] affectivity, love, or desire might also
> be an occasion to somewhat reevaluate our criti-
> cisms of "mushy" worship choruses that seem to
> confuse God with our boyfriend. While we might
> be rightly critical of the self-centered grammar of

such choruses, I don't think we should so quickly
write off their "romantic" or even "erotic" elements (the Song of Songs comes to mind in
this context). . . . The quasi-rationalism that
sneers at such erotic elements in worship [and]
is concerned to keep worship "safe" from such
threats is the same rationalism that has consis-
tently marginalized the religious experience of
women—and women mystics in particular.

You might disagree with that observation. And I don't
want to suggest that enchantment demands that we
shelve our critical faculties when it comes to the theological content of praise music. I'd love it if theologians
and artists collaborated more in writing worship songs.
What we're talking about here is how excessive rationality *amputates our hearts in worship*, crippling our ability to
pray and sing. Which can affect anyone, men or women.

Enchantment involves reconnecting your head with
your heart. I think Pascal is exactly right. It is the heart
that experiences God. Faith is a largely emotional, even
romantic, affair. If you're struggling with the spiritually corrosive effects of excessive rationality, let me recommend the enchantments of charismatic worship, no
matter where you go to church. When it's time to sing,
sing. And sing loudly. Open your heart. Surrender to the
praise. Move. Dare to raise your hands. Or kneel during

prayer. You're not a computer. Let your body confess and your emotions embrace the truth that your mind cannot. Faith isn't an accounting problem; it's a romance. So when that Holy Ghost conga line starts up, jump in and join the dance.

11

CELTIC
ENCHANTMENTS

Patrick stood on the shore. The cold winds snapped at his cloak, the uneasy sea roiled behind him. His gaze stared out over a land that once had been a nightmare. Hope for the future mixed with haunted memories. He had returned to the land of his bondage and slavery.

At the age of sixteen, in fourth-century Britain, Patrick had been kidnapped from his home and taken to Ireland as a slave. There he worked as a shepherd in the lands of Miliucc, an Irish lord who ruled lands between Lough Neagh and the mountains of Sliabh Mis. For six years, Patrick labored as a slave tending sheep in hungry isolation, cut off from home and daily companionship.

In his loneliness and isolation, Patrick began to pray. And through his daily communion with God, a change was wrought. Against all odds, a season of bondage became a season of spiritual transformation. As Patrick recounts in his *Confession*, "When I had arrived in Ireland and was spending every day looking after flocks, I prayed frequently each day. And more and more, the love of God and the fear of him grew in me, and my faith was increased and my spirit was quickened, so that in a day I prayed up to a hundred times, and almost as many in the night. Indeed, I even remained in the wood and on the mountain to pray. And—come hail, rain, or snow—I was up before dawn to pray." The enslaved shepherd boy was slowly becoming a saint.

After years of prayer, the voice of God spoke to Patrick: "Well you have fasted. Very soon you are to travel to your homeland." Soon after, the voice spoke again: "Behold! Your ship is prepared." Taking this as divine permission to escape his master, Patrick abandoned his sheep and made the two-hundred-mile journey to meet the ship divinely appointed to return him home to Britain.

While Patrick's reunion with his family was joyful, he soon realized he was a man out of place. His six years of prayer and fasting—through rain and snow, in woodlands and on mountains—had changed him. He found his heart haunted by the people he left behind in Ireland. One night, a vision came to Patrick of a man he knew from Ireland. In the dream, the Irishman handed Patrick a large stack of letters. Patrick opened a letter and read the top line: "The Voice of the Irish." The pile of letters contained the cries of the lost souls in Ireland, begging for Patrick to return. As Patrick shares in his *Confession*, the voices in the letters "were shouting with one voice: O holy boy, we beg you to come again and walk among us."

It would be a few years before Patrick would return as a missionary to the people of Ireland. After his visions, he sought training and ordination to be a priest and eventually became a bishop. But Patrick would heed the "Voice of the Irish." He returned to the land of his exile to bring Christ to the Celts.

The land Patrick gazed upon when he stood, once again, on the shore of Ireland was a pre-Christian world of pagan, Celtic spirituality, a world of druids, stone circles, nature spirits, and magic. *Celts* was a catchall name for the tribal peoples Romans encountered in central Europe on the western flank of their empire. Some of these Celtic tribes had made their way to the British Isles during the Iron Age. Linguistic similarities between the Irish, Welsh, and Scottish languages point back to these Celtic settlers.

The Celts were eventually "Romanized" when Rome came to rule much of Britain by 87 CE. And along with Rome eventually came Christianity, a process hastened by the conversion of the Roman emperor Constantine. After Constantine made Christianity the official religion of the Roman Empire, Roman Britain soon became Roman Catholic Britain.

But Roman rule and Christianity didn't make it to every part of the British Isles. To the north, Scottish tribes held off Roman incursion, causing the Roman emperor Hadrian to build a wall from the North Sea to the Irish Sea, effectively sealing off the Scottish tribes to the north. Rome also never successfully conquered Ireland. Thus while most of Britain came under the influence of both Rome and the Catholic Church, Ireland and Scotland were left to themselves, their tribal and Celtic ways and beliefs continuing on outside of Roman and Christian influence. Celtic ways and beliefs also persisted in Wales and Cornwall, the extreme western reaches of Britain.

I go into all this history to draw something important to your attention. When Patrick sailed back to Ireland, he was stepping into a wholly alien world. Where the Celtic tribes of Britain had been both Romanized and Christianized, the Celtic tribes of Ireland had been left undisturbed. The faith Patrick was bringing to the Celts was foreign to them. For the first time in the history of the world, Christianity would clash and mix with a spirituality that hadn't been shaped by a prior Roman occupation and influence. Even St. Paul, the first and greatest Christian missionary to the pagan world, had depended on Rome. To spread the gospel, Paul relied on Roman law, peace, commerce, language, and most importantly, Roman roads. Patrick, by contrast, as he stood on Ireland's shore, was attempting to do something that even Paul hadn't dared to try: to take the message of

Christ beyond the boundaries of the Roman empire. The Romans had a name for the wild, barely human peoples who existed beyond the walls of their empire—*barbarian*. Pagan though they were, Paul preached to the Romans. But in becoming a missionary to the Celts, Patrick would do something unprecedented in Christian history.

Patrick was going to evangelize the barbarians.

In the unprecedented challenge Patrick faced, there was also the possibility for something novel and new. Prior to Patrick, in the West, Christianity had always been planted and grown in Roman soil. Christianity was *Roman* Christianity. Patrick's mission would give birth to a Christianity cultivated and fertilized in non-Roman soil, a *Celtic* Christianity. Patrick might have been the first missionary in the West to a non-Roman people, but he wasn't the last. Christianity has always mixed and fused in creative, interesting ways with indigenous spiritualities. Patrick brought about just such a fusion—what we call Celtic Christianity—when he returned to Ireland to share the message of Christ.

Against the odds, Patrick's mission was wildly successful. A Celtic-flavored Christianity flourished in Ireland, and Patrick would go on to become *Saint* Patrick, patron saint of the Irish. In the generations after Patrick, Irish monks would leave their homeland to establish monastic communities in Iona and Lindisfarne, bringing their unique spirituality to Britain. And beyond Britain, Irish monks like Brendan and Columbanus would bring a Celtic-inspired Christianity, along with their illuminated codices, to Europe.

The heyday of Celtic Christianity came to an end with the Viking invasions of the British Isles. In the face of the repeated plundering, the Celtic monks finally gave up and abandoned Lindisfarne in 875 CE. This was followed by the Anglo-Norman invasion of Ireland in 1170, effectively bringing an end to any ongoing and distinctive Irish influence upon Western Christianity. However, starting around 432 CE, when Patrick returned to Ireland, for almost five hundred years, a unique flavor of Christianity emerged and flourished among the Irish and their monks. And this Celtic Christianity has bequeathed to us rich resources for modern Christians searching for enchantment.

Before digging into the enchantments of Celtic Christianity, I need to stop and say something about objections that might call the entire notion of "Celtic Christianity" into question.

The first objection concerns the commercialization of Celtic Christianity. Basically, "Celtic" is a bit of a brand. Slap a Celtic knot or cross or an Irish blessing on something, and you can sell it as "Celtic." Likewise, in the realm of faith and religion, you can slap "Celtic" onto almost any spiritual mumbo jumbo and sell that as well. There's a ton of books on the market selling "Celtic" versions of Christianity and spirituality, many full of rubbish and caring little about historical accuracy. Anything vaguely spiritual or mystical can get branded as "Celtic." To avoid this, I've taken care to make sure that all the Celtic poems and prayers you read in this chapter come from historical Celtic sources. No mumbo jumbo, I promise.

Which brings us to a second, more scholarly concern. Almost everything about the Celts and Celtic Christianity is controversial and disputed. Many scholars contend that the "Celts" never really existed, not as a culturally and ethnically identifiable people. Another example: almost everything about St. Patrick can trigger an academic temper tantrum. Some scholars, though in the clear minority, question if St. Patrick even existed. Others have also argued that the "Celtic versus Roman" church contrast is too simplistic and distorting. The Roman and Celtic streams bled into and influenced each other, it is argued, making them impossible to disentangle. Many speakers, gurus, artists, and authors like to contrast a freer, more spiritual, more egalitarian, more environmentally friendly "Celtic" Christianity with a more dogmatic, rigid, patriarchal, and hierarchical "Roman" Christianity. Scholars think that contrast is way too simplistic or just plain wrong. As St. Patrick himself once said to the Celts, "If you would be Christians, then be as the Romans."

These objections duly noted, most scholars agree that the Christianity that emerged from Patrick's Ireland did have a distinctive quality, texture, and sensibility. These qualities can be found elsewhere within the Christian tradition, so we need to avoid simplistic, unwarranted contrasts. For example, the Desert Fathers were hugely influential upon the Celtic saints. Much of what gets branded as "Celtic" can be found throughout the Christian tradition. But the contrasts people make about Celtic Christianity haven't emerged out of nowhere. Scholars have long recognized distinctive features that characterized Irish monasticism, a unique spiritual sensibility we can gather under the label "Celtic Christianity." The particular texture of this spirituality can be gleaned by reading the poems, prayers, sermons, devotions, and liturgies of the early Irish Christian tradition along with the lives of the Irish saints. This distinctive Celtic spirituality is also communicated through the art and artifacts the Irish Christians bequeathed to us, from the high crosses of Ireland to the illuminations of *The Book of Kells*.

We should keep a critical eye out whenever we hear something marketed to us as "Celtic," but anyone can read the Celtic breastplate prayers—the most famous being St. Patrick's—and see there's something unique going on in this neck of the Christian woods. You experience the peculiar strangeness of Celtic Christianity when you hear St. Columba opine, "Jesus is my druid." Or learn about the Celtic *caim* prayers, prayers of protection offered to the Trinity as one draws a circle of protection around oneself to ward off dark, occult forces. If all that sounds a wee bit magical, well, it is. That's why we're here. With the Celtic tradition, we are, most definitely, in a unique neck of the Christian woods. And who isn't up for a walk in an enchanted forest?

Or hunting for magic eels?

The spirituality of the Celts expressed an affinity for place. Pre-Christian Celtic rituals took place in glades, by rivers, or on mountains. Celts also gathered at places where ancient peoples had erected standing stones, the most famous of these being Stonehenge. These local shrines, presided over by druids, were liminal "thin spaces," enchanted, magical places where the boundary between the spiritual and physical worlds was permeable or nonexistent. The Celtic Christians retained this enchanted sensibility in regard to place. And they weren't stingy in this regard. High crosses sprouted up across the Irish landscape, each location declared holy, enchanted, and sacred. The numerous holy wells found throughout the British Isles are another example of the promiscuous Celtic tendency to enchant place. You'll recall my search for magic eels at the holy well of St. Dwynwen. The day after our visit to Llanddwyn Island, we went to—wait for it—Holywell to visit St. Winefride's Well. Called the "Lourdes of Wales," sick pilgrims seeking healing have been bathing themselves in St. Winefride's Well since the twelfth century. Holy wells are found throughout the British Isles, so many they are almost commonplace. Every village seems to have a holy well, a testament to the Celtic willingness to anoint small, local spaces as hallowed and sacred.

This holy willingness to anoint the place where you stand as sacred is a gift of the Celtic tradition, the Celtic sensibility that any place can be a "thin space" where God is encountered. All it takes is a little willingness to see. Like Jacob, we find ourselves in the middle of nowhere special and suddenly realize, "This is the gateway to heaven!"

This Celtic interest in place is really just a particular example of the Celtic tendency to enchant all of nature. Of all the enchanted Christianities we've surveyed, it's the Celtic tradition that takes particular delight in creation, experiencing God in an encounter with the natural world. Among the Celtic Christians, there is an erotic joy and sensuous delight in the natural world that can strike more pious ears as borderline pagan. There are temptations here that we need to pay attention to, but it's hard not to smile at the Celtic Christian delight in the sheer sensuality of human life. Try to keep from smiling as you read the Welsh poem "The Loves of Taliesin":

The beauty of berries at harvest time,
Beautiful too the grain on the stalk.
The beauty of the sun, clear in the sky . . .
The beauty of a herd's thick-maned stallion,
Beautiful too the pattern of his plaits.
The beauty of desire and a silver ring,
Beautiful too a ring for a virgin.
The beauty of an eagle on the shore when the tide is full,
Beautiful too the seagull's playing . . .
Beautiful too a generous and obliging minstrel.
The beauty of May with its cuckoo and nightingale,
Beautiful too when good weather comes.
The beauty of a proper and perfect wedding feast,
Beautiful too a gift which is loved.
The beauty of desire for penance from a priest,
Beautiful too bearing the elements to the altar.
The beauty for a minstrel of mead at the head of the hall . . .
The beauty of a faithful priest in his church . . .
The beauty of the moon shining on the earth,
Beautiful too when your luck is good.
The beauty of summer, its days long and slow,
Beautiful too visiting the ones we love.
The beauty of flowers on the tops of fruit trees,
Beautiful too covenant with the Creator.
The beauty in the wilderness of doe and fawn,
Beautiful too the foam-mouthed and slender steed.
The beauty of the garden when the leeks grow well,
Beautiful too the charlock in bloom . . .

The beauty of the heather when it turns purple,
Beautiful too pasture land for cattle.
The beauty of the season when the calves suckle . . .
And for me there is no less beauty
In the father of the horn in a feast of mead.
The beauty of the fish in his bright lake,
Beautiful too its surface shimmering.
The beauty of the word which the Trinity speaks,
Beautiful too doing penance for sin.
But the loveliest of all is covenant
With God on the Day of Judgment.

I don't know who Taliesin was, but the guy had a sacramental imagination. Every moment, sight, and small pleasure—from mead to good music—was a "thin space," a moment of enchantment, God everywhere present. Celtic spirituality is a world-affirming, life-affirming, body-affirming, pleasure-affirming spirituality. An old Irish sermon describes the kingdom of heaven this way: "The kingdom of heaven [is like] summer and fair weather, flower and leaf, beauty and youth, feasts and feasting, prosperity and an abundance of every good thing."

Beyond the words of "The Loves of Taliesin," the poetry itself, as a form of spiritual insight and communication, is also a distinctive characteristic of Celtic spirituality.

Among the Celtic Christians, the poets stepped into some of the social roles previously filled by the druids as repositories of oral traditions. As Oliver Davies has noted, "The religious poetic tradition in both Wales and Ireland is one of the most important sources for Celtic Christianity since it was an area of Christian culture that continued to represent a vital point of contact with cultural and religious paradigms that belonged to an earlier pre-Christian world." The Celts believed poets to be uniquely positioned to receive and communicate spiritual truths. For the Celtic Christians, the Holy Spirit was the source of poetic inspiration. As one Celtic poem says, "Poetry's welfare is in Elohim's care."

If enchantment involves a recovery of a sacramental imagination, the Celtic tradition illustrates how *poetry is a spiritual practice* and a resource for re-enchantment. Where the contemplative tradition gives us *prayer* as a practice of attention, the Celtic tradition gives us *poetry*. Poetry sees the world through enchanted eyes, bringing into view the deeper meanings, signs, and mysteries at work in everyday things. Reading and writing poetry is practicing a sacramental imagination.

Related to the Celtic embrace of nature, Celtic Christianity also held the spiritual power and potency of women in high regard. This strong affirmation among the Celtic

Christians of "the sacred feminine" is, no doubt, another example of pre-Christian influences. Among the pre-Christian Celts, the earth was associated with fertility, nurturing, and maternal powers. So it's no surprise that the Celtic Christians, in their embrace of nature, would have a great sacramental regard for women and mothers. The Celts saw male and female as one among many sacred opposites found in nature. An example of these "sacred opposites" comes from a Celtic poem in praise to the Trinity:

> He made Mars and Luna,
> Man and woman,
> The difference in sound between
> Shallow water and the deep.
> He made the hot and the cold,
> The sun and the moon.

This sacramental view of femininity and motherhood should not be strange to the Catholic and Orthodox traditions, given their strong devotion to Mary, who is honored as "the Mother of God" and Theotokos ("God bearer"). The Catholic and Orthodox traditions are also full of powerful, miracle-working women. Among the Celtic Christians, St. Brigit of Kildare looms large. Patron saint of Ireland alongside Patrick, Brigit founded two hugely influential monasteries in Kildare and held jurisdiction over much of southwest Ireland. In what appears to be a scandalous Celtic innovation, one of Brigit's monasteries was for women and the other for men. To account for her leadership over male monastics, one tradition about Brigit was that she was "accidentally" anointed as a bishop. Various accounts of Brigit's life also blend elements of Christian hagiography with pagan motifs of sacred femininity and goddess worship. This blending is visible in Ireland to this day. St. Brigit's feast day, February 1, is the same day as the pagan festival of Imbolic, a celebration linked to pre-Christian fertility rituals and the coming of spring.

It would be foolish to believe that the Celts and the Celtic Christians practiced a radical egalitarianism or feminism when it came to gender roles. However, as seen in the St. Brigit tradition, many tout Celtic Christianity as an alternative to more patriarchal expressions of Christianity. I bring up the Celtic sacramental view of femininity and motherhood to make an observation about enchantment. Celtic Christianity's happy inclusion of feminine and maternal elements in their sacramental imagination (and I'd include here the Marian devotions of the Catholics and Orthodox, along with their prayers and devotions offered to female saints) can help us with re-enchantment. This is especially true for Protestant traditions that are almost wholly devoid of feminine imagery.

Maternal imagery, of either God or nature, emphasizes nurturing and mothering. This sacramental and devotional imagery places us in a needy, dependent, and childlike posture in relation to God and the world. Stepping into this imagination, we stop viewing ourselves as autonomous, separate, isolated, and self-sufficient. This sacramental imagery of dependency is an *enchanted* posture because, once again, it is an *eccentric* posture: as a needy child, we see the lie of self-sufficiency. We confess that we cannot exist alone in isolation from the Source that gives us life. Dependency embodies the outward turn as we look for succor, care, affection, love, and nurturing *from the outside.* Dependency enchants because it is the ache and need that causes us to search for and lean upon God. Maternal imagery for God focuses our attention on our childlike dependence as we gaze into the face of the God who is our Mother. Psalm 131 (NIV) beautifully expresses the Celtic sentiment:

> *My heart is not proud, Lord,*
> *my eyes are not haughty;*
> *I do not concern myself with great matters*
> *or things too wonderful for me.*

> *But I have calmed and quieted myself,*
> *I am like a weaned child with its mother;*
> *like a weaned child I am content.*

Before moving on, I think it's important to share some clarifications about the life-affirming, body-affirming, and pleasure-affirming impulses within Celtic spirituality. A lot of misunderstandings and mischaracterizations arise at this point, so a clearer, broader picture of Celtic spirituality needs to be painted. Given the nature-affirming spirituality we observe in verses like "The Loves of Taliesin," Celtic Christianity is often accused of being a baptized paganism. There is a lot of stuff on the market under the label "Celtic Christianity" that really is just pop paganism for Christians. And it can be hard to tell the difference. There's a delicate balance between recognizing nature as sacred and worthy of reverence and outright nature worship. But anyone who reduces Celtic Christianity to nature worship has woefully misjudged the Irish saints.

While the Celts reveled in the natural world, they were keenly aware that it was *Christ* who was surrounding them in all of creation. Creation isn't the divine Presence; creation *mediates* the divine Presence. Creation is holy and sacred because it is *Christ* who comes to us in the rain, sun, and wind. There is no better example of Christ's sacramental presence in the world than the famous breastplate prayer of St. Patrick:

Christ with me, Christ before me, Christ behind me;
Christ within me, Christ beneath me, Christ above me;

Christ to the right of me, Christ to the left of me;
Christ in my lying, Christ in my sitting, Christ in my rising;
Christ in the heart of all who think of me,
Christ on the tongue of all who speak to me,
Christ in the eye of all who see me,
Christ in the ear of all who hear me.

Consider also lines from another Celtic prayer:

The path I walk, Christ walks it. May the land in which I
am be without sorrow.
May the Trinity protect me wherever I stay, Father, Son,
and Holy Spirit.
Bright angels walk with me—dear presence—in every
dealing.

The Celtic Christ is the Christ of the apostle Paul: "For in [Christ] all things in heaven and on earth were created, things visible and invisible . . . and in him all things hold together" (Colossians 1:16–17). Christ is in all things—in rock, leaf, water, and wind—holding everything together. The Celtic Christians would have heartily agreed with Gerard Manley Hopkins that "Christ plays in ten thousand places." Wherever you go, the dear presence is felt. Bright angels walk with you.

We also need to reject equating Celtic Christianity with sentimental nature worship because of its very high view of the Christian ascetical tradition. The Celtic

Christians adored and emulated the Desert Fathers, with their severe fasting, penances, and mortifications. Let's not forget the young St. Patrick praying outdoors during rainstorms. The Celtic monks reveled in nature, but they regularly sought harsh, forbidding locations in which to live. And lacking caves like their heroes the Desert Fathers, the Celtic monks built austere beehive-shaped cells out of stacked rocks. There is a life-affirming sensuality to Celtic spirituality, but Celtic Christian practice was also disciplined and ascetical. Beyond enjoying mead and good music, "The Loves of Taliesin" also praises the "desire for penance" and looking forward to Judgment Day. Like the druids before them, the Celtic saints were spiritual sages who could both heal and curse. And similar to the Desert Fathers, the spiritual potency of the Celtic holy men and women was directly related to the severity of their ascetical practice. The Celtic saints who most severely mortified and disciplined themselves were the ones with the greatest miracle-working powers. For the Celtic Christians, enchantment wasn't just a frolic among the shamrocks. Magic implied mortification. Enchantment flowed out of ascetical discipline.

The ascetical aspect of Celtic spirituality provides us with another resource for enchantment. Celtic Christianity loves food, but it also loves to fast. The Celtic Christians called these ascetical practices the "green martyrdom." (The Celtic word here is *glas*, which could be translated as "green" or "blue." Most translators go with "green martyrdom," but you sometimes see it translated as the "blue martyrdom.") An old Celtic sermon describes the green martyrdom as "fasting and hard work," through which Christians "control their desires or struggle in penance and repentance." Never forget that Ash Wednesday is just as Celtic as Fat Tuesday.

On the surface, it might seem that ascetical disciplines such as fasting go against the Celtic embrace of the body. But if fasting is anything, it's an *embodied* spirituality. As anyone who fasts regularly can tell you, fasting makes you *more* aware of your body, not less. Hunger keeps the soul tethered to the body. In fasting, physical hunger and spiritual hunger merge together in prayer. Given that enchantment is a practice of attention, where we bring to mind spiritual realities, ascetical practices like fasting are some of the biggest tools at our disposal.

The ascetical practices of the Celtic Christians also help us practice enchantment as *recovery*. Ascetical practices recover bodily gifts as *gifts*. As J. R. R. Tolkien described, the gifts and pleasures of life—mead and good music—come to be taken for granted over time. We grow bored and indifferent. We stop paying attention to leaf and flower, to the touch of sun upon our skin. Both habit and overindulgence numb the senses. In a strange psychological paradox, pleasure is tied to rarity. We love an exquisite meal precisely because we don't get to have it every day. If we did, we'd tire of it quickly, no matter how good it was. Pleasures are delightful indulgences to the degree that we discipline ourselves, holding them off and setting them apart as special splurges and treats. From food to sex, by checking excessive consumption, ascetical practices do not deny bodily pleasure; they enchant. We recover pleasure as a blessing and gift.

Reveling in nature and the life of the body as good gifts given to us by God was a break between the Celtic Christians and the magical, occult, and druidic practices of the pre-Christian Celts. Though the druids and their nature worship did leave a distinctive mark on Celtic Christianity. Consider the blending of Christian and druidic influences in this Celtic prayer:

> *I beseech you, Father. I beseech you . . .*
> *Every angel, every song, every creature under your power, every saint of fair color, by them I beseech you, O Father. I beseech you.*
> *I beseech you by time with its clear divisions, I beseech you by darkness, I beseech you by light.*
> *I beseech all the elements in heaven and earth that the eternal sweetness may be granted to my soul.*
> *Your infinite pity, your power over battles, your gentleness to your debtors, O beloved and swift King.*

To help me out in every conflict, by them I beseech you, O
   Father.
I beseech you.

There's a druidic whiff about the prayer, beseeching "all the elements in heaven and earth." But a break is occurring as well. The appeal to the created order is directed ultimately toward God, who is not compelled to answer. That is the pathos of the prayer, the *beseeching*. This isn't a magical incantation; it's a prayer for help. As the druids were replaced by the Irish monks and saints, a shift in the Celtic imagination occurred regarding their relationship with nature. Nature was no longer viewed as being "charged" with elemental powers that could be harnessed and manipulated through druidic ritual and magical arts. Creation was, quite simply, a gift. The natural world was sacred because it was graced. The breeze, rain, trees, and starlight were to be received with childlike wonder, joy, delight, and gratitude. Nature became the kiss of God. No longer viewed as a source of power to be magically controlled, creation became a *blessing*, a gift to be simply affirmed and enjoyed. And enjoy it they did! With hearts full of gratitude. Among the Celts, spells and incantations gave way to hymns of praise and thanksgiving:

From God I beseech guardianship of the gift
Of praising my generous and gracious Lord,
Mary's single son who makes morning and afternoon,

And fertile stream,
Who made forest and field and true measure,
Fruit and God's abundant gifts,
Who made grass and trees, heather on the hills . . .

But let's also not imagine that the Celtic Christians experienced nature as tame and benign, full of rainbows and daffodils. This is another common mischaracterization of Celtic Christianity and a lesson we learned from the charismatics. Life is a long moral struggle, and the world is full of dangers. Among the most common and distinctive of the Celtic prayers were the lorica prayers. *Lorica* is Latin for "armor" or "breastplate." Lorica prayers were "protection prayers," which took their cue from Ephesians 6: "Put on the whole armor of God, so that you may be able to stand against the wiles of the devil. . . . Stand therefore, and fasten the belt of truth around your waist, and put on the breastplate of righteousness." The Celtic tradition is chock full of breastplate prayers, each requesting divine protection from misfortune, illness, injury, and malevolent attack, from both natural and supernatural enemies. Again, Saint Patrick's Breastplate is the most famous example:

I rise today
with the power of God to pilot me,

God's strength to sustain me,
God's wisdom to guide me,
God's eye to look ahead for me,
God's ear to hear me,
God's word to speak for me,
God's hand to protect me,
God's way before me,
God's shield to defend me,
God's host to deliver me,
from snares of devils,
from evil temptations,
from nature's failings,
from all who wish to harm me,
far or near,
alone and in a crowd.

Around me I gather today all these powers
against every cruel and merciless force
to attack my body and soul,
against the charms of false prophets,
the black laws of paganism,
the false laws of heretics,
the deceptions of idolatry,
against spells cast by witches, smiths, and druids,
and all unlawful knowledge that harms the body and soul.

May Christ protect me today
against poison and burning,

against drowning and wounding,
so that I may have abundant reward.

As we've seen, the enchanted self was experienced as "porous," vulnerable to outside forces in the world, usually supernatural and occult powers. There's no better example of this vulnerability than the Celtic breastplate prayers. In the enchanted Celtic world, the self could get possessed, hexed, cursed, or jinxed. Protection was very much needed.

This Celtic concern over dark, occult forces at work in the world is similar to the charismatic concern about spiritual warfare. Both spiritualities have a porous, enchanted experience of the self, a self that is vulnerable and in need of divine protection. Again, for skeptical and disenchanted Christians, this vulnerability will seem strange. Few of us woke up to face the day with the words "Lord, protect me from the black laws of paganism and against the spells cast by witches, smiths, and druids." As Charles Taylor said, our modern experience of the self is "buffered," a self that stands alone, autonomous, and isolated, walled off from the outside world. This buffered self doesn't need protection. But it's precisely here where the Celtic breastplate prayers can help us. Prayers of Help recover enchantment because they draw our attention *away from autonomy and self-sufficiency* to focus on our *vulnerability*. When we hold this vulnerability before God in prayer, our experience becomes more Celtic and enchanted. We practice this vulnerable, enchanted self when we rise with St. Patrick to pray each morning, "May God's strength sustain me, God's wisdom guide me, God's hand protect me, God's shield defend me."

When you spend time with Celtic Christianity, you also notice a sociability that is often lacking elsewhere in the Western monastic tradition. I suspect it has to do with the Irish being Irish. But whatever the reason, with their love of mead and good music, the Celtic Christians delighted in human community and friendship.

One Celtic contribution concerning the importance of spiritual fellowship and friendship is the *anam cara*, the "soul friend." *Anam cara* is an Anglicization of the Irish word *anamchara*, *anam* meaning "soul" and *cara* meaning "friend." The "soul friend" comes from the Irish monastic tradition, where monks would seek spiritual guidance and support from wise, compassionate counselors. For the Irish monks, having an anam cara in your life was vital for spiritual and emotional flourishing. The Celtic saints needed their friends. As St. Brigit once said to a young monk under her care, "Anyone without a soul friend is like a body without a head."

The anam cara of the Celtic tradition highlights another important truth about enchantment: God comes to us through our "soul friends." We've been talking a lot about how our dependency and vulnerability places us in an eccentric posture, looking for help outside of ourselves. The Celtic tradition teaches us that God comes to us in leaf, flower, and rain. But God also comes to us in flesh and blood, in our anam cara. When Patrick prays "Christ with me, Christ before me, Christ behind me, Christ to the right of me, Christ to the left of me," that presence comes mostly through our soul friends, the people blocking for us, watching our backs, and holding our hands. Enchantment comes to us through other human beings. Our eccentric outward turn is often toward each other. Especially when life is hard and we begin to waver and doubt. I like how Dietrich Bonhoeffer describes what soul friends do for each other:

> God has willed that we should seek and find God's living Word in the testimony of other Christians, in the mouths of human beings. Therefore, Christians need other Christians who speak God's Word to them. They need them again and again when they become uncertain and disheartened because, living by their own resources, they cannot help themselves without cheating themselves out of the truth. They need other Christians as bearers and proclaimers of the divine word of salvation. They need them solely for the sake of Jesus Christ. The Christ in their own hearts is weaker than the Christ in the word of other Christians.

Their own hearts are uncertain; those of their brothers and sisters are sure.

When our hearts are uncertain, and when we are cheating ourselves out of the truth, grace and truth come to us on the lips of our soul friends. Once again, help comes to us from the outside.

As you know, Hannah, Jana, and I didn't find the magic eels on Llanddwyn Island. But it was good to be in Celtic Wales with Hannah and some other soul friends. After exploring the ruins of the abbey and the Celtic high cross, Hannah, Katrina, and Llewellyn went for a swim. Jana, JoJo, and I found ourselves sitting on the dunes, wind in our hair, staring out over the water.

Wales is a very enchanted place. Especially when you're visiting one of those magical "thin spaces," sites of Celtic devotion and pilgrimage. It's easy to feel the sacred rhythms of the ancient Celts while sitting on the sand of Llanddwyn Island or visiting St Winefride's Well. But resting on the dunes that day with Jana and JoJo, a truth hit me: the Celts weren't on vacation. This island was their home. And they filled it with wonder and magic.

Here's our problem: it's easy to experience enchantment on vacation. Anyone can feel a bit Celtic visiting Ireland or Wales. Anyone can feel closer to God on a beach or hiking in a national park. I don't want to dismiss the restorative, spiritual magic of these beautiful places. We need these natural wonders and how they help us find God in nature. Redwood forests are life changing, inspiring, and holy. So is Llanddwyn Island. But if we only experience the enchantment of the natural world on vacation, I think we've missed the lesson the Celtic saints were teaching us. West Texas, where I live, is a long way from Wales. And way less enchanted, in the opinion of many people. Tumbleweeds aren't as magical as shamrocks, I guess. But no matter where you live, the encouragement of the Celtic saints is this: enchant the place where you find yourself, right where you are standing. "Lord of all places," the Celtic Christians prayed, "how good you are to praise."

This is an enchanted world. God is the "Lord of all places." In West Texas, in Wales, and where you are sitting right now. So let's all declare, like Jacob, that *our place*—right here, right now—is the gateway to heaven. No matter where you find yourself, in sunshine and in rain, the grace of God enchants the day. Christ plays in ten thousand places, even here in West Texas. As a Celtic poet wrote,

> *On the hill and in the valley,*
> *On the islands of the sea,*
> *Whichever path you take,*
> *You shall not hide from blessed Christ.*

12

THE PRIMACY OF THE INVISIBLE

Let me put two images in front of you. First: an enormous tree wrapped in foil.

On the evening of September 9, 2021, a thunderstorm passed through Sequoia National Park. A lightning strike ignited a fire. The flames grew, spread, and became the KNP Complex Fire, which soon threatened the sequoias of the "Giant Forest." Like the redwood trees I described in chapter 2, sequoias are some of the largest and oldest trees in the world. Among the sequoias threatened by the KNP Complex Fire was the 275-foot tree named "General Sherman," the largest tree in the world.

Acting to save General Sherman and other sequoias, firefighters and park rangers took an unusual action. They wrapped the enormous trees in foil. Well, not foil exactly, but large, aluminum blankets to protect the trees from the heat and flames.

Hold that enormous, foil-wrapped sequoia in your mind.

My second image comes from the end of the first year of medical school. By far, the most demanding class of the first year is a course called "Gross Anatomy." In Gross Anatomy, medical students are given a donated body to dissect across the entire year. The class is the cornerstone of medical training, giving students an intimate knowledge of human anatomy. Students dissect everything, examining the brain, the heart, the lungs, the stomach, the intestinal tract. Nerves, bones, muscles, and joints. Head to toe, sternum to spine.

The experience of a gross anatomy class, as you can imagine, is very scientific and clinical. The human body becomes an object of minute empirical observation and inspection. And while that investigation is vital for medical training, there's also something deeply unsettling about reducing a once-living human being to tissues and bones. In the face of that spiritual dissatisfaction, a widespread tradition in medical schools has been to hold services honoring the people who donated their bodies to the class. Next to a foil-wrapped tree, that's the second image I want to put before you: this ceremony during medical school.

These two images communicate a truth that Joseph Ratzinger, Pope Benedict XVI, described as "the primacy of the invisible." The most *important* thing about a tree like General Sherman is *invisible*. What is invisible about that tree causes us to wrap it up in foil. The invisible is an orbit of value, a gravity well of meaning, that pulls us in and compels a moral response. These invisible ligaments of meaning and value penetrate and saturate every nook and cranny of existence. Like a vast, shimmering spiderweb. We sense the vibrations in this web of meaning and rush to save the sequoias. An invisible reality is constantly tugging on the material world.

That same tugging creates rituals of honoring among medical school students for the donated bodies of a gross anatomy lab. Close, clinical dissection of the human body will never bring this invisible pull into view. A wholly materialistic analysis of organs, bones, nerves, and tissues cannot see what demands sacred recognition. Right there—sitting at the heart of an objective, clinical, surgical experience—enchantment reigns. The holy takes its place in the center of the room and we are called to respond. And what is true in a gross anatomy lab is true everywhere. What is *primary*—what is most important in our lives—is *invisible*.

Enchantment is always at hand. Marilynn Robinson once described it like this:

Ordinary things have always seemed numinous to me. One Calvinist notion deeply implanted in me is that there are two sides to your encounter with the world. You don't simply perceive some-thing that is statically present, but in fact there is a visionary quality to all experience. It means something because it is addressed to you.

We're switching the metaphor from seeing to hearing, from the primacy of the invisible to being "addressed" by creation. The world is speaking to us. The psalmist describes it in Psalm 19:

> The heavens are telling the glory of God;
> and the firmament proclaims his handiwork.
> Day to day pours forth speech,
> and night to night declares knowledge.
> There is no speech, nor are there words;
> their voice is not heard;
> yet their voice goes out through all the earth,
> and their words to the end of the world.

The disenchanted cosmos is mute. Silent and quiet. But for the enchanted, the sequoias are speaking. The bodies in gross anatomy labs are speaking. Everything in heaven and on earth is speaking. We are being addressed by the world.

The Jewish theologian Martin Buber describes being "addressed" as having an "I-Thou" encounter. According to Buber, experience comes in one of two types, "I-It" or

"I-Thou." In an I-It encounter we experience the world as an "it," as an inert, static object. I-It experiences are nonrelational because the "it" is impersonal and lifeless. True relationship happens, according to Buber, when we encounter a sacred presence, a "Thou." As Marilynn Robinson described, there are two sides to every encounter: I-It and I-Thou, disenchanted and enchanted, silence and speech. The world is not simply "statically present" before us; we are being "addressed" by a sacred presence. "All real living is meeting," said Buber. Enchantment is an encounter. We cover trees in foil because a *relationship* exists between us and the sequoias. A relationship that demands holy recognition.

But for many, the universe is falling silent. We're increasingly trapped inside our own skulls as the outside world becomes lifeless and dead. We look toward the heavens and hear . . . nothing. No speech. The world is becoming an "it."

The sociologist Hartmut Rosa has attempted to describe this silencing of experience. "The fundamental fear of modernity is fear that the world's falling mute," he says. "Modernity stands at risk of *no longer hearing the world.* . . . Modernity has lost its ability to be *called,* to be *reached.*" (The emphases are his.) Our increasingly scientific and technological I-It relation to the world, says

Rosa, is actually "a relation of relationlessness"—which
is to say, no relationship at all. Rosa's work is an attempt
to discover how we can restore "a successful relationship
to the world." Rosa describes this successful relationship
as one of "resonance," a sympathetic, harmonious, and
responsive connection with all of life.

As described by Rosa, this resonant I-Thou relationship has four characteristics. First, we can be *affected* by
the world. We can be "reached, touched, or moved" by
the encounter. We hear a call. Next, we *respond* to the
call. This response can be emotional or behavioral. We
see such a response in the firefighters who wrap sequoias
in foil. Third, we can be *changed* by the encounter. Think
of Thomas Merton on Fourth and Walnut. The experience changed his life, setting the cloistered monk on a
path of activism. Sacred meetings can leave a permanent
mark. We become "a different person." And lastly, as I
described in chapter 4, these encounters cannot be controlled by us. An I-Thou encounter is open-ended and
unpredictable. The relationship cannot be forced. Yet, all
around us we see the dark desire to "manage" the world.
And this, argues Rosa, is a key reason the world is falling
silent:

> Modernity is culturally geared and, given how
> its institutions are designed, structurally driven
> toward making the world calculable, manage-
> able, predictable, and controllable in every

possible respect. Yet resonance cannot be made controllable through scientific knowledge, technical mastery, political management, economic efficiency, and so on.

We are being driven from an I-Thou relationship to an I-It relationship with life, driven from enchantment into disenchantment. The more we try to control—through science, technology, politics, and economics—the more the world falls silent.

All the enchantments we've explored in part 3—liturgical, contemplative, charismatic, and Celtic—are attempts to retore us to a "successful relationship to the world," a richly resonant and enchanted relationship. What all these enchanted traditions have in common is how they address our attention blindness. I can't keep stressing this point enough: Resonance isn't achieved through an act of willpower. It won't be forced. But we can start paying attention.

In his book *The World Beyond Your Head*, Matthew Crawford observes that the word *attention* comes from the Latin root *tenere*, which means "to stretch and make tense." Attention creates a contact point with the world beyond our heads, making a connection with a reality other than our own. Given that tether of attention, tension between two realities is established and we are drawn out of ourselves and into a relationship. What is lacking in the disenchanted experience are these attachment points, tethers of attention that draw us out into "the world beyond our heads." Each of the enchanted Christianities described in part 3 provides a rich variety of attachment points to draw us into relationship with a larger reality.

In contrasting the power of attention over willpower, I've been struck by an observation made by novelist and philosopher Iris Murdoch. Her observation concerns how we overcome or change strong emotions. But her point is just as applicable to faith in a disenchanted age. Murdoch writes,

> Where strong emotions of sexual love, or of hatred, resentment, or jealousy are concerned, "pure will" can usually achieve little. It is small use telling oneself "Stop being in love, stop feeling resentment, be just." What is needed is a reorientation which will provide an energy of a different kind, from a different source. Notice the metaphors of orientation and of looking. . . . [Changing ourselves] is not a jump of the will, it is the acquiring of new objects of attention and thus of new energies as a result of refocusing.

Let me rephrase Murdoch's quote to make the point about faith:

> Whenever we experience religious doubts or have crises of faith, "pure will" can usually achieve little. It is small use telling oneself "Stop having doubts! Believe! Have faith!" What is needed is a reorientation which will provide an energy of a different kind, from a different source. Notice the metaphors of orientation and of looking. Faith is not a jump of the will, it is the acquiring of new objects of attention and thus of new energies as a result of refocusing.

This is precisely how the enchanted traditions of Christianity help us. You can't force a belief. Rather than a "jump of the will," faith is nurtured by "the acquiring of new objects of attention." Through these practices we are pulled out of ourselves, drawn back into life with an expectation of encounter. Experiences resonate. What was once invisible slowly comes into view. And a silent world begins to speak.

PART 4

DISCERNING THE SPIRITS

13

ENCHANTMENT SHIFTING

Something has been dogging us. A question I floated early on that you might have wanted to insert into the conversation: Are we really as disenchanted as I've been making it out?

It's a great question. The assumption we've been working with is that Western civilization has been on a journey, moving from an enchanted experience of the world toward a secular, scientific, skeptical, and disenchanted world. But many have called this enchantment-to-disenchantment story into question, naming the tale the "myth of disenchantment." You can see their point. People still believe in ghosts and magic. Fewer people might be traditionally "religious," but many readily describe themselves as "spiritual." When people turn away from traditional religious observance, they don't generally opt for atheism. They dabble in crystals, herbs, oils, meditation, yoga, astrology, and New Age spiritualism, shopping around to forge their own unique path forward. Nothing could be more American than this "design your own" approach to religion and faith.

This raises two issues that we need to squarely face and deal with.

I've been suggesting that we need to recover "eccentric experiences" with God in this skeptical age. We need to pay more attention to our mystical and spiritual encounters with God. We *believe* in God because we've *encountered* God. We've turned aside, like Moses, to behold the strange sight and stand on holy ground. Nothing could be more in tune with the times, in this "spiritual but not religious" climate, than this focus upon personal encounters with God. So is that what I've been talking about, calling for a more "spiritual" and less "religious" Christianity?

The answer is yes and no. I am calling us toward a more mystical and experiential Christianity. But there are dangers and temptations here that need to be addressed and resisted. If we're not very careful, a more "spiritual" Christianity can quickly devolve into something spacey and sentimental. In 1 John 4:1, we are warned, "Beloved, do not believe every spirit, but test the spirits to see whether they are from God." If our faith is to pay more attention to spiritual and mystical experience, then it also has to be equipped to "discern the spirits." There's a bunch of strange, wacky stuff out there in the spiritual marketplace. A lot of it is just baptized self-indulgence, a quasi-mystical gloss we use to mask our selfishness and consumerism. "Spirituality" is a brand and product in America. If we are paying more attention to the "strange sights" around us, we have to be equipped to suss out the kookiness and the self-centeredness.

What about the "myth of disenchantment"? Are we really as disenchanted, doubting, and skeptical as I've suggested? The answer, again, is both yes and no. Friedrich Nietzsche was really naming something in the modern world when he declared that "God is dead." The Christian faith is in obvious decline in the West. Rates of agnosticism and atheism, along with the nones, continue to rise. Even among the faithful, we can see the effects of disenchantment. Sermons about the most enchanted aspects of the Christian life, like belief in heaven, have been disappearing from our pulpits. For many of us, Christianity has to make sense here and now, on this earth. This isn't the case in every church, but if you pay attention, you can see the effects of disenchant-ment among Western Christians: much less talk about the more enchanted aspects of our faith—heaven, mir-acles, the devil—in favor of things that we can see and touch, from social justice to the emotional support we give each other within a faith community.

Disenchantment is a force; it's not a myth. You see its effects everywhere and feel them in your heart whenever you question the existence of God, miracles, or the reality of heaven or recall all the nagging doubts that haunt your faith. But the critics do have a point. Dogmatic atheists are in the minority. Most people are supernaturalists. We believe we have a soul and that our deceased loved ones "watch over us." We believe in miracles, angels, ghosts, and karma. Even when people don't believe in God, they believe in some "higher power," convinced that there is something more going on in the universe than the sum of its subatomic parts.

It's a complicated, even paradoxical, picture. One way to make sense of what's going on is that we're not just witnessing the effects of disenchantment, a rising tide of disbelief. We're also watching *a shift of enchantments*. The two can look a lot alike. When we watch church attendance decline, we might assume this reflects rising disbelief. But more often than not, people are turning to different, non-Christian enchantments, the "spiritual but not religious" phenomenon. A prior *religious* enchantment hasn't turned into disbelief; it has shifted into a *spiritual* enchantment. Disenchantment is on the rise, but enchantments have also been shifting. Paying attention to this "spiritual but not religious" shift is going to be critical if we want to "discern the spirits." God is speaking to us, but it's awfully noisy out there.

On the evening of October 27, 312 CE, two armies spent an uneasy, restless night. In the morning, they would meet in open conflict on the shores of the Tiber, near the Milvian Bridge on the outskirts of Rome. Every soldier in the rival camps knew the fate of the Roman Empire hung in the balance. But more than the fate of Rome was on the line. The next twenty-four hours would determine the fate of the entire world.

Constantine had come to Rome to remove his brother-in-law Maxentius in a bid to claim sole rule over the Roman Empire. The day before the battle, while marching with his troops, Constantine looked at the sun and saw a sign. Above the sun was the image of a cross, with words emblazoned in light, "Through this sign, you will conquer." The pagan emperor was uncertain about the meaning of the vision, but the following night, on the eve of battle, he dreamed a dream. In the dream, Christ directed Constantine to use the sign of the cross to defeat Maxentius. Heeding the vision, Constantine directed his soldiers to paint the Chi-Rho symbol upon their shields. An early Christian symbol, the Chi-Rho was made through the intersection of the letters chi (X) and rho (P) from the first two letters of the Greek word *Christos*, the name of the Christian God.

Marching to war under the sign of Christ, Constantine won the Battle of the Milvian Bridge to become the sole ruler of the Roman Empire. The aid Constantine received from the Christian God during that battle would go on to play a pivotal role in the pagan emperor's conversion to Christianity, along with his eventual estab-lishment of Christianity as the official religion of the Roman Empire. Constantine's vision before the Battle of the Milvian Bridge would prove to be a decisive moment in world history. The Roman world began its conversion to Jesus Christ, turning away from the ancient gods.

As the official faith of Rome, Christianity began to displace and replace the paganism that had held sway since the dawn of history. While the Christian church grew in power and influence, the temples of Zeus, Mars, Apollo, and Athena fell into disuse and ruin. Through-out the empire, pagan priests found themselves jobless. It wasn't just the gods of Olympus who were displaced; everywhere Rome ruled, Christian missionaries, priests, and monastics established churches and monasteries, all with the goal of converting the barbarians to the worship of the Christian God. Eventually, in one of the most seis-mic shifts in world history, Christianity came to dominate the entire Western world, a cultural and political influ-ence that continues to this very day. Globally, over two billion people today identify as Christian, making it the largest religious group in the world. Temple sacrifices to Zeus are a thing of the past. The triumph of Christianity over paganism appears to be complete.

But appearances can be misleading. The ancient gods and rituals of Greece and Rome are no longer forces in the world today, but paganism continued to exist and thrive on the margins of Christendom. Despite Christian influence and power, popular interest in the occult, spiritualism, astrology, and magical lore never really waned, not then and not now. Christianity might have won the political battle against paganism, but it never fully won the cultural battle. From the fourth century on, the political rulers of the West were Christian. But that political triumph didn't translate into a complete societal transformation. Our planets still carry the names of the Roman gods—Mars, Venus, Jupiter—and Thursday is named after Thor, the Norse god of thunder. Christianity itself became a repository and guardian of paganism, as many pagan celebrations and traditions were simply co-opted and rebranded by the church, allowing pagan festivals and feasts to carry on uninterrupted.

Paganism and Christianity have existed side by side for over two thousand years, each presenting themselves as live options for those seeking enchantment and an encounter with the sacred. Today, as the influence of the church wanes in the post-Christian West, paganism is thriving and experiencing a cultural revival. After two thousand years of Christian cultural dominance, enchantment is shifting again in the West. Paganism is back.

But we're not seeing temples being built to Zeus in town squares or witnessing our neighbors burning animal sacrifices in their backyards. The conclusion "paganism is back" seems a bit premature.

It all depends, really, upon how we define and describe paganism. Traditionally, paganism referred to polytheism, believing in a multitude of gods, in contrast to the monotheism of Christianity, Judaism, and Islam. Pagans believed in gods, while monotheists believed in God. But this has always been, right from the beginning, a fuzzy distinction. Christians believed in a Creator God and vowed to worship Him alone, but they also believed that the spiritual realm was buzzing with spiritual beings and powers, like angels and demons. Nor did being a monotheist mean you stopped believing in sorcery or ghosts. Christian monotheism changed how people worshipped, but their vision of the supernatural world didn't change all that much from their pagan forebears. Christians worshipped God, but the supernatural realm they inhabited was as busy and bustling with spiritual and magical powers as it had always been.

But something did change with Christian monotheism. A decisive break with the pagan past was made. Christianity didn't reduce the number of spiritual powers, spirits, and forces inhabiting the world, but it did shift pagan enchantment toward a new and different experience of the sacred.

Steven D. Smith describes the contrast between pagan and Christian enchantment as less concerned with the number of the gods than a difference in *the location of the sacred*. Smith makes the contrast, "If we understand religion as a relation to the sacred . . . then pagan religion differs from Judaism and Christianity in its placement of the sacred. Pagan religion locates the sacred *within* this world . . . it is a religiosity relative to an *immanent* sacred. Judaism and Christianity, by contrast, reflect a transcendent religiosity; they place the sacred, ultimately, *outside* the world." In paganism, there are a variety of spiritual and elemental energies, potencies, and forces flowing throughout the natural world. These powers are sacred energies that enchant and sacralize creation, but these powers and forces are a part of the created order. Pagan enchantment is an *immanent* enchantment, which is to say the natural world is inherently and intrinsically sacred; the magic is found organically within the elemental forces, spirits, and powers of the world. Christian enchantment, by contrast, locates the sacred not within creation but in the *Creator*. Christian enchantment is a *transcendent* enchantment; the magic is located beyond and above creation. Christians do not worship created things, even if they are powerful elemental spirits or forces. Throughout history, Christians might have continued *believing* in these spirits and forces, but they no longer *worshipped* these powers. The opening lines of the

Ten Commandments held sway: "I am the Lord your God . . . you shall have no other gods before me. You shall not make for yourself an idol, whether in the form of anything that is in heaven above, or that is on the earth beneath, or that is in the water under the earth. You shall not bow down to them or worship them" (Exodus 20:1–5). This was the fundamental shift from pagan to Christian enchantment, locating the sacred in the Creator rather than within the created order. In his letter to the Romans, Paul makes the contrast between the immanent enchantments of paganism and the transcendent enchantment of Christianity: "Ever since the creation of the world [God's] eternal power and divine nature, invisible though they are, have been understood and seen through the things he has made. So they [the pagans] are without excuse; for though they knew God, they did not honor him as God or give thanks to him, but they became futile in their thinking, and their senseless minds were darkened. Claiming to be wise, they became fools; and they exchanged the glory of the immortal God for images resembling a mortal human being or birds or four-footed animals or reptiles" (Romans 1:20–23).

But as Paul points out, this distinction between immanent and transcendent enchantments isn't so clear-cut. God reveals Himself through the created order, making His invisible attributes visible in the goodness of nature and human life. The immanent enchantments of Christianity were also the focus of Paul's first sermon to the pagans in Acts 14, where he described God as the one who fills us with good food and our hearts with joy. God is in these creational gifts, but we don't worship the earth for the harvest. We direct our thanks to the Creator God who speaks to us and cares for us in and through our bodies and the blessings of the natural world. As we've discussed, the natural world is sacred in being *sacramental*, as an enchanted sign pointing us toward the God who cares for and loves us. This sacramental quality of creation is beautifully captured in a passage from St. Augustine's *Confessions*:

> "But what is it that I love?" I asked the earth, and the earth replied, "It is not me," and all that lives upon the earth declared the same. I asked the sea and its depths, and all the reptiles living there, and they replied, "We are not your God. Seek Him above us." I asked the blowing winds, and the air and all that lives within it replied, ". . . I am not God." I asked the sky, the sun, the moon and the stars, and they replied, "Nor are we the God you are seeking." And I said to all the things outside the gates of my flesh, "Tell me of that God you are not. Tell me something about Him." And in a mighty voice they all cried out, "He made us."

This was how Christianity shifted pagan enchantment. Creation was no longer worshipped as a god nor the elemental powers within creation worshipped as deities. Creation, instead, became a *gift*, an experience of *grace* from the One who made us and fills us with joy. Nature is a sacrament and conduit of grace. All the wonders of the world point toward God and declare, "He made us!"

If Christianity shifted pagan enchantment toward the transcendent, today we are experiencing a shift back toward a more immanent enchantment. The beauty and wonder of the natural world are increasingly seen as sacred *in themselves* and *all by themselves*. So are the pleasures of the body, the joys of mead and good music. In the self-description "spiritual but not religious," we are embracing a more pagan experience, locating the sacred organically within the natural world. Notice, for example, how the labels *natural* and *organic* have become signposts of enchantment in our post-Christian world, the sorcery of our skeptical age. The word *organic* infuses food with mystical potency, and all that is *natural* is sacred and good.

Stepping back, this is how enchantment has been changing in the modern world. The transcendent enchantment of Christianity has been both *waning* and *shifting*. Alongside rising disenchantment, the immanent enchantments of paganism, which have endured and thrived through centuries of Christian dominance, are experiencing a resurgence and renaissance.

This might not seem like a big deal. Enchantment is enchantment. Being spiritual seems better than being nothing at all. Why should anyone care about a loss of transcendent enchantment?

Let me start by saying some positive things about the immanent enchantments of paganism, the good fruits of the "spiritual but not religious" crowd. There are many places where the pagan and spiritual folk put us Christians to shame. Pagans are often more Christian than the Christians.

For example, the transcendent enchantment of Christianity, seeing the sacred as "above and beyond" the natural world, has tempted the church, right from the start, into a world-hating, pleasure-denying, nature-destroying Gnosticism. The Gnostics were early Christian heretics who claimed that the created world and the body were bad. Only the spiritual was considered pure, holy, and good. For the Gnostics, the goal of the spiritual life was to deny the physical body and escape the natural world to attain a wholly spiritualized existence. You can see how a transcendent enchantment—the sacred placed *outside* of and *beyond* creation—could be tempted in this way. If the spiritual should not be contaminated by the physical, then the entire natural world becomes 100 percent disposable and discardable. In addition, those Celtic pleasures of mead and good music, the physical joys of the body, become highly suspect and problematic. These Gnostic temptations continue to haunt us whenever we see Christians defend the destruction and exploitation of the natural world or puritanically wring hands whenever anyone is having a good time.

What the Gnostics lost track of, as many Christians still do today, was the *immanence* of Christian enchantment, God's presence in all things, how matter matters. When that happens, when Christians become overfocused upon transcendence, they become, in the words of the old song, "so heavenly minded they are no earthly good." They can also do great harm.

Because it locates enchantment immanently, pagans have tended to have a much better witness when it comes to caring for, protecting, and stewarding the environment. When it comes to loving God's "very good" earth, as Genesis 1 declares, pagans frequently put Christians to shame. Christians can learn much about their own faith by attending to how pagans encounter the sacred in the natural world.

But transcendence does matter.

The reason transcendent enchantment is falling out of favor in our world is that we don't much like the sacred standing "over and above" us. A transcendent enchantment creates the possibility for judgment and critique, that our lives could be *evaluated* by a God who is watching over us. That notion, that we could be, in the words of Daniel 5, "weighed on the scales and found wanting" is simply intolerable to modern people. We are the captain of our own ship, and the only truth that can stand in judgment of us is the truth we chose for ourselves. We don't need a God in the heavens bossing us around and telling us what to do. We are the ones we've been waiting for.

Transcendent enchantment challenges the central conceit of the modern world, that no one, not even God, can stand in judgment of us. So it's not surprising that immanent enchantment is now all the rage on the spiritual marketplace. One of the most noteworthy features of modern-day "spirituality" is how eclectic it is, how you *choose* it. In the modern spiritual marketplace, you *pick* your enchantment, like shopping for deals at Walmart. Dabble in astrology or sign up for a yoga class. Explore Kabbalah or buy some crystals. Burn some sage or practice meditation. Pick your magic, black or white? Here are some herbs and essential oils. Make a shrine to the god or goddess of your choice. Shop for aromatherapy candles. Mix and match until you achieve the enchantment perfectly suited for your lifestyle, budget, political views, values, and friend group. All fit to order.

There are blessings in herbal remedies. Peace is found in meditation. And joy comes to us in the physical exertions of our yoga class. These things aren't problematic in themselves. But immanent enchantments are *collected* and *curated*, the product of our whims and fancies. Our enchantments have become *lifestyle choices*. We pick the enchantment that suits us or is most in fashion. Or the one we can afford. And celebrities are such a help here. Enchantment becomes a brand and fad, the mystical tinsel we sprinkle over our curated images on social media.

If we're thoughtful, we can sense the shallowness of it all. Can an enchantment we pick up and lay down at a whim really give our lives the sacred meaning and weight we've been longing for? Can an enchantment we choose for ourselves become anything but narcissistic, a reflection of our own highly selective and cropped self-image? Immanent enchantments are on the rise because they are perfectly suited to our consumeristic age. And that is the fatal, fundamental flaw.

Let's also rush to confess that transcendent enchantments are also vulnerable on this score, how we use God to justify our vices, meanness, selfishness, political views, national interests, and greed. Just because the enchantment is "above and beyond" us doesn't mean we're immune to the temptation to use God to baptize our vanity, selfishness, thirst for power, and prejudice.

The critical issue, then, for both the religious and the spiritual alike, is this: Can your enchantment judge, criticize, and unsettle you? Can your enchantment point out your selfishness and self-indulgence? Can your enchantment, be it burning sage for your spell or singing "God Bless America" in your pew, hold a mirror up to your hypocrisy? Can your enchantment weigh your nation or political party on the scales and find it wanting? Does your enchantment create sacrificial obligations and duties in your life that you cannot avoid or ignore? Does your enchantment call you to extend grace to people you'd prefer to hate? Does your enchantment bust up your cozy self-satisfaction and dogmatic self-righteousness?

These are questions that won't be asked by an enchantment bought on Amazon. This fierce and honest moral examination can only be conducted by an enchantment that is "over and above" us, an enchantment that can *judge* us and hold our feet to the fire, an enchantment that cannot be avoided or blown off like the latest fad. These are the questions we have to ask when we seek to "discern the spirits," when we want to determine if the voice we are hearing is from God or from our own egos.

When it comes to enchantment, let's dare to ask ourselves the hard questions. God is speaking to you when you feel the sand under your feet on vacation and when you have that magical evening with your friends, full of feasting and laughter. But there is a danger in experiencing God *only* in these locations. It's always a bad sign when you have to spend money to experience God, on either airfare or alcohol. And it's not a good sign when we only care for the people who look, think, and vote like we do. God comes to us in beautiful locations and people, in restorative places and safe spaces. But a truly transcendent enchantment is going to nudge us out of our comfort zone. The gate of heaven is everywhere, even in the boring, the difficult, the hard, and the ugly.

Perhaps it is true that we aren't as disenchanted as we think we are in this skeptical age. Enchantment is everywhere you look. The magic is for sale and trending on Twitter. And we're tempted to shop around. But if you're looking for the "strange sight," longing to hear the voice of God in this "spiritual but not religious" marketplace, slow down and take some care. Discern the spirits. Spiritual and religious people alike. Enchantments are shifting, and if we're not careful and paying close attention, we're going to end up worshipping ourselves.

14

HEXING THE TALIBAN

In August of 2021, as American military forces were evacuating Afghanistan, a controversy broke out on WitchTok. WitchTok, in case you didn't know, is the witchcraft community on the social media platform TikTok. Over the last few years, social media has witnessed the rapid growth of spaces devoted to paganism, the occult, magic, and witchcraft. Documenting this rise, in 2020 *The Atlantic* ran an article titled "Why Witchcraft Is on the Rise." That same year *Wired* declared, "TikTok Has Become the Home of Modern Witchcraft (Yes, Really)." A year later, the *New York Times* asked, "When Did Everyone Become a Witch?"

Like I said, paganism is back.

The controversy on WitchTok in the summer of 2021 concerned the movement "Hex the Taliban." Concerns about the Taliban were understandable. As Taliban forces retook Afghanistan, countless people around the world grew concerned about the plight of women in that country. Would women be forced into marriages with Taliban fighters? Would girls be able to go to school under Taliban rule?

Taking action, the witchcraft community on social media gathered forces for a mass hexing of the Taliban. That mass hexing caught a lot of attention, but controversies broke out when some "baby witches" (new, novice, and inexperienced witches) attempted to escalate the confrontation. Some baby witches were skipping the Taliban, wanting to go right to the top. Some baby witches wanted to hex Allah.

The witchcraft community is metaphysically diverse. There is no settled consensus about what witches believe. Overall, hexing the Taliban appeared to have the approval of much, if not most, of the witchcraft community. But when attempts were made to hex Allah, some disagreements emerged. And those disagreements illustrate the metaphysical distinctions I drew in the last chapter, the difference between immanent and transcendent enchantments.

As debated among the witchcraft community, the central controversy surrounding baby witches trying to hex Allah concerned safety. Given Allah's power, was hexing Allah too dangerous? Some witches who made the attempt believed so, and shared their experiences. One witch on social media warned, "Do NOT face Allah alone when Astral projecting," reporting what transpired on the astral plane:

> Today while astral projecting I summoned Allah to try and weaken him so our hexing spells would work better.
>
> He is so f------ powerful. I'm not at a power level to do this alone. I barely escaped with my life. . . . I can't imagine what he would do to a new, unsuspecting witch. . . . Please be safe everyone. Allah is much stronger than I first imagined and we will have to do this together if we want to slay a god.

The heart of the debate in the witchcraft community, concerning whether Allah is too powerful to hex, is what I'd call a "video game metaphysics," a "Dungeons & Dragons metaphysics," or even a "Marvel Cinematic Universe metaphysics." In this imagination there exists a hierarchy of power. Normal people, like me, are low on this power ranking. More powerful than regular people are those who possess "super" or "magic" powers. Witches have such powers. So do sorcerers and wizards in role-playing games. So do the superheroes in Marvel movies. Above these powerful humans are more and more powerful beings, like demigods. As we keep powering up, we reach the gods. And maybe, at the very top, we reach God, like Allah or Yahweh. The Most Powerful Being in the Cosmos.

I call this power hierarchy a "video game metaphysics" because video games often culminate in what is called a "boss fight" at the end of the game. Role-playing games and superhero movies have similar boss-fight endings. Early on in the game, campaign, or movie the threats are small and less powerful. Weaker minions of the Big Boss. The player or superhero fights through these weaker enemies to finally come face-to-face with the Big Boss, the most powerful foe. The game, campaign, or movie ends by defeating this most powerful opponent in a big, climactic boss fight. The entire imagination of these games and movies is moving up through a hierarchy of power.

This depiction of the hierarchy of power reached its pop-culture zenith with Thanos in the Marvel movies *Avengers: Infinity War* and *Avengers: Endgame*. By himself, Thanos was pretty powerful. But when Thanos collected all six Infinity Stones—the Space Stone, the Reality Stone, the Power Stone, the Mind Stone, the Time Stone, and the Soul Stone—combining them into the Infinity Gauntlet, Thanos could, with a simple snap of his fingers, do anything imaginable. Thanos could snap the cosmos out of existence, and back into existence. Or snap a wholly different reality into being. Thanos with the

Infinity Gauntlet is the most powerful being we humans can imagine.

This Marvel Universe vision of power is how the witches on TikTok imagined the confrontation with Allah. Like Thanos with the Infinity Gauntlet, Allah was a very powerful Boss. So, a novice or less powerful witch would need to "power up" if they were to challenge a being so high up the power hierarchy. And from the perspective of this "video game metaphysics," such advice seems reasonable. You could understand why experienced witches were warning baby witches about the advisability of hexing Allah alone.

The problem, though, was that the witches weren't really talking about God.

Let me stipulate that while there are fundamental disagreements between Christianity, Islam, and Judaism, the three Abrahamic and monotheistic faiths are all speaking about the same God when they name Allah, Yahweh, or God. All three faiths are speaking of the Creator, the one who calls being into existence *ex nihilo* ("from nothing"). Simply, *God* names the reason there is something rather than nothing.

To describe God as the One Who Creates Ex Nihilo is to describe God as *transcendent*, as fully *beyond* and *outside* the created order. As the Source of the cosmos, God cannot be located *within* the cosmos. If the cosmos is a very large room, God cannot be located among the furniture of that room. Neither is God to be found in a different room were we able to travel there. God does not live in Asgard like Odin or on Mount Olympus like Zeus. God is not locatable in the cosmos like Odin, Zeus, or Thanos. God is not a Big Boss.

The trouble with the WitchTok debate about hexing Allah is that it was confused about who God is. The problem wasn't that hexing Allah was dangerous, that Allah was too powerful. The problem was that the WitchTok community was assuming that God, the witches, the astral plane, and their hexes all existed within the same order of being. Each at different power levels, yes, but still existing in such a way that contact could be made between them. But this "video game" view of God is metaphysically confused. God is the Source of Being, which means that God "exists" in a way wholly different from how Odin, witches, or hexes exist. If hexes exist at all, and let me grant for the sake of this argument that they do, the problem with hexing God isn't that God is too powerful for a baby witch, but that God is what makes baby witches and hexes exist in the first place. A hex cannot affect the Source that brings it into existence and holds it in being. Hexes aren't weak in relation to God's power. They cannot even "make contact" with God within the same plane of existence. Hexes and God exist *differently*. Trying to hex God is like throwing a rock into space. You're not going to hit anything.

This is also a point that needs to be raised with atheists. I've talked enough with atheists to understand some of their common retorts and arguments. Many atheists are just as confused as WitchTok.

For example, atheists will often say, "As a Christian, you don't believe in Odin. I, as an atheist, don't believe in your god." They might also bring up the Flying Spaghetti Monster, or compare God to a supersized teapot orbiting the earth. (Google it.) These fantastical objects have been used by atheists over the years to argue for God's nonexistence, or to shift the burden of proof for God's existence onto believers. But these arguments miss the point. The problem with the Big Boss imagination of WitchTok is the same problem here: God is not an object that can be found within the universe. As the Source of Being, God cannot exist as either a monster or a teapot. God is the reason for existence itself.[1]

---

1 If you were wondering, this discussion explains how God's *transcendence* doesn't create a two-story universe but, rather, God's *immanent presence* in our one-story universe. Simply, it is God's *transcendence* that allows God to come *close*. Theologians call this God's "non-competitive relation" to the world. Because God exists differently than created things, God doesn't compete for space in our world. For example, if God were an object within the world, existing as we exist, as a piece of furniture in the house of the cosmos, God would have to jostle and compete for space alongside us. Where God took up space I would be shoved aside, the same way you and I can't stand in the same spot. But since God exists *differently*, God doesn't compete for space with us or with

Of course, this clarification of terms is no proof of God's existence. All we are doing is clarifying what we mean by the word *God*. If by *God* you mean an object within the universe (even an object on the astral plane), an object like Thanos, Odin, a Flying Spaghetti Monster, or a giant teapot—well, I have news for you: That's not God. Not as Christians understand God. But if by *God* you mean the Source and Reason for existence itself, the Being in which beings have their being, now we're talking about the same thing. You don't have to believe in God, but you're starting to use your words correctly.

Before moving on, while we're here talking about immanent and transcendent enchantments, I'd also like to make a point about magical systems.

As lovers of fantasy know, the magical systems we find in fiction and movies can be either hard or soft. Soft magical systems are vague and undefined. How the magic "works" is hidden from us. Soft magic is used by authors to evoke wonder, surprise, and awe in the worlds they create. The entire world is filled with enchantment. *The*

---

anything in creation. It's God's transcendence that allows God to be *immediately* and *intimately* present to all things, everywhere and always, in a non-competitive, non-shoving relationship. This is why, as Augustine famously observed, God is closer to you than you are to yourself. Or as Thomas Merton said, you cannot be without God. It is impossible.

Chronicles of Narnia and *The Lord of the Rings*, produced by two Christian authors, are examples of soft magical worlds. And that's no surprise, as Christian enchantment, our sacramental ontology, is akin to a soft magical experience. God is present and filling all things, and we expect the magic to show up everywhere. The world is full of wonder and awe, charged with the grandeur of God. There is a visionary quality to all experience.

Witchcraft, by contrast, traffics in hard magic. Hard magic is rigid and rule based. Hard magic is a metaphysical tool, a bit of supernatural technology. It's right there in the words: witch*craft* and spell*casting*. The heart of magical practice is the hex or spell, a technique used to influence and control metaphysical powers and potencies. As Ambrosia Hawthorn writes in *The Spell Book for New Witches: Essential Spells to Change Your Life*, "[Spells] work by manipulating energy to fulfill a specific intention or purpose. . . . It's through this manipulation that you can influence or control the energy around you." Notice all the mechanical words: *manipulation, influence, control.* This is hard magic. Magic you can use to get things for yourself. The spells in *The Spell Book for New Witches* are categorized in parts like "Romantic Love," "Money Matters and Prosperity," and "Work and Career." To pick a spell at random from *The Spell Book for New Witches*, consider the technology at work in the "Fidelity Ring Charm." This spell "enchants commitment rings to inspire trust between you and your partner." The charm is "intended for use on wedding bands, but can be used on any jewelry." Ingredients for this spell include a tablespoon of carrier oil, pink pillar candles, one teaspoon of dried basil, one teaspoon of licorice root, and two pieces of jewelry. The spell should be performed during the spring equinox, summer solstice, or a waxing moon. The spell is estimated to take about fifteen minutes, and begins with these steps:

1. Cleanse your altar.
2. Pour the carrier oil onto a plate.
3. Lay the pillar candle in the oil and roll it back and forth.
4. Sprinkle the basil and licorice root over the rolled candle until it's lightly coated on all sides . . .

And so on. The spell is to be repeated every one to three months to "recharge the pieces."

My point isn't to make fun of the "Fidelity Ring Charm," though it's a weird sort of fidelity if you have to hex your wedding rings every three months. My point, if you've never seen a spell book, is to show how witchcraft is a practice of *technology*, a tool to *manipulate* the world. And truth be told, there is much within Christianity that is a similar practice of hard magic. The prosperity gospel movement, with its "name it and claim it" practices of invoking God to secure wealth and influence, looks a lot like the hard magic of *The Spell Book for New Witches*. God is being used as a tool to accomplish our purposes in the world. And the prayer requests of the prosperity gospel movement look exactly like the table of contents in the spellcasting books: a list of petitions for romance, wealth, career success, and health.

But the enchantment of faith is a soft magical world. The enchantment of faith is beauty, grace, wonder, and joy. Christian enchantment isn't a *technology*. Christian enchantment is a *relationship*. That's what I wish the witches knew about transcendent enchantment. Enchantment isn't an energy to be manipulated or a spell to be cast. Enchantment is being carried by the Love that is the very Source of your being, the Love that holds your every breath and heartbeat in a loving embrace. I wish the same for my brothers and sisters in the prosperity gospel movement. The enchantment of prayer isn't asking Thanos to snap his fingers to give us what we want. Christian enchantment seeks God's *presence* more than God's power. God is not Santa Claus and our prayers are not spells. Beware when Christians turn soft magic into hard, when prayer becomes less about relationship with God and more about getting something we want.

I'm putting the metaphysics of WitchTok under the microscope because a criticism of this book has been its strong focus on disenchantment. We have, here in part 4, turned to face that issue, the "myth of disenchantment." Most people are supernaturalists. We aren't as skeptical and unbelieving as some have claimed. WitchTok is an excellent example of this, the rising visibility and influence of paganism on social media. So, in light of this pagan resurgence, it's worth giving more attention here in this chapter to the differences between transcendent and immanent enchantments. If only to help clear up some of the metaphysical confusions on WitchTok.

Consider two lovely tables from Skye Alexander's book *The Modern Guide to Witchcraft: Your Complete Guide to Witches, Covens, and Spells*, named by *Wicca Living* as a top introduction to witchcraft. Chapter 6 of *The Modern Guide to Witchcraft* is devoted to "Gods and Goddesses." Right out of the gate, we're introduced to what I described in the last chapter about immanent enchantments: You get to pick and choose your own. Enchantment shopping! Alexander writes, "Witches, Wiccans, and Neopagans . . . often disagree about the nature of the divine. . . . Who or what you believe in—if anything— is totally up to you." It's like a Dungeons & Dragons game. Choose your own adventure. Pick a god or goddess of your choice. You can believe in any of these gods, or none of them. Doesn't really matter. Totally up to you.

From Alexander's table of goddesses we can pick, among many others, Artemis (a Greek goddess of courage, independence, and protection), Freya (a Norse goddess of love, healing, and sensuality), and Yemaja (a

Nigerian goddess of secrets, dreams, childbirth, and purification). Among the gods, we can choose from Ganesh (an Indian god of strength and overcoming obstacles), Pan (a Greek god of nature and fertility), and Thoth (an Egyptian god of knowledge, science, and the arts), among others. Again, you don't have to believe in any of these gods or goddesses. The tables just give you some ideas. Totally up to you.

Let's say you decide to believe in Loki, because Loki's cool and you like Tom Hiddleston. Having started to believe in Loki, you can call upon him for help. As Alexander encourages, "Want to take a trip? Invite Mercury to help you plan your itinerary. Need some extra power on the gridiron? Consider adding Mars or Mithras to your team. . . . If you are facing a big challenge or obstacle, you could call on the Hindu god Ganesh to assist you. Perhaps you admire a certain deity's attributes and want to add them to your own character. If you'd like to be more compassionate, say, you could align yourself with Kuan Yin, the Asian goddess of mercy." The immanent enchantments of paganism are perfectly suited to this sort of "choose your own" spirituality, tailor-made to fit to our wishes, desires, politics, and personality type. And there are no strings attached. You can return any of these gods and goddesses for a full "refund" and start believing in different ones. As *The Modern Guide to Witchcraft* encourages, who or what to believe in—if anything—is totally up to you.

This consumeristic approach to enchantment extends even into morality. Just as you can pick your own god, you're free to pick your own ethics. I recall encountering the moral diversity of paganism during my chaplaincy training at the prison where I lead a Bible study. As a state institution, our prison provides programming for all religious groups. Years ago, bewildered by the diversity of the pagan groups, the state of Texas attempted to gather them all under the single heading "Neo-Pagan." Trouble was, the Wiccans and the followers of Odinism hated each other and couldn't peaceably share the same space for religious services. Odinism, the state of Texas discovered, is a white supremacist faith, which the Wiccans strongly objected to.

Personally, I'm with the Wiccans on this one. But the dispute between these pagan faiths highlights the moral incoherence of immanent enchantments, how you pick your own vision of good or evil. And while I appreciate the nonjudgmental attitude of paganism, at the end of the day good and evil cannot be determined by the choice of a consumer. Good and evil aren't products you buy, open to return if you're unhappy with your purchase. But that consumer-driven approach sits at the heart of witchcraft's choice between black and white magic, between the Wiccans and the Odinists.

That there's even a distinction between white and black magic reveals a metaphysical confusion. A contrast between white and black magic can only exist if there is

some moral vantage point standing in judgment of magical practices. We're back to a transcendent enchantment
that morally classifies how we use our hexes, sorting
them as either black or white based on the "Love Wins"
standard we've inherited from Christianity. And if we
lose this transcendent evaluation, then anything goes,
morally speaking. Black is just as good as white, and there
is no reason to object to the white supremacy of Odinism
or to the Taliban refusing to let young girls go to school.
Magic might be comforting and fun, but it is too consumeristic to help us confront the injustices of the world.

Still, I was deeply sympathetic to the WitchTok community during the American withdrawal from Afghanistan.
I was also worried about the Afghan women and girls as
the Taliban took over the country. We both cared about
the women of Afghanistan. Christians and witches were
allies in that concern.

Truth be told, perhaps the main reason witchcraft is
on the rise, among women especially, is due to the oppres-
sions women have faced at the hands of the Christian
church, past and present. From the burning of witches
to the abuses exposed by the #ChurchToo movement,
women have suffered at the hands the church. Fleeing
that oppression, women and girls have turned to pagan
spiritualities that center "the divine feminine." As a

response to oppression, witchcraft is often more *political* than *metaphysical*. And insofar as the witchcraft community is speaking a prophetic word against the oppression of women in Christian spaces, I think they are doing the Lord's work. Sometimes, as I've said, the pagans are more Christian than the Christians.

Even so, a deep metaphysical difference separated how WitchTok and I saw the moral crisis in Afghanistan. I believed then, as I do now, that the oppression of women is *transcendentally* wrong. I firmly believe this is the *truth*. You don't get to approach oppression as a consumer, opting for either good or evil. You can't say "It's totally up to you" when it comes to hurting women. There is a transcendent moral truth at stake, and you don't get to choose what to believe. The truth is the truth. It's true for Christians. True for witches. True for Odinists. True for me. True for you. And true for the Taliban.

And no god you can pick from a table is going to be able to secure this truth. Only God can do that.

15

GOD'S ENCHANTMENT

The ring cut through the still night. Martin quickly got up, hoping to get to the phone before it awakened his sleeping wife and daughter. Reaching for the receiver, Martin lifted it and placed it to his ear. It was around midnight.

"Hello?"

A low, menacing voice answered back, "N—, we're tired of your mess. And if you aren't out of this town in three days, we're going to blow up your house and blow your brains out."

Shaken by the phone call, Martin found his way to the small kitchen. He'd received threats before, but they had been mostly bluster. Something in this voice was different. The call wasn't a scare tactic. This voice was speaking the truth, making a promise. Whoever made that call was going to try to kill him and his family.

He hadn't signed up for this, a new husband and father taking death threats in the middle of the night. When he moved to Montgomery to become the pastor of Dexter Avenue Baptist Church, he was looking forward to a quiet, scholarly life. Only twenty-five years old when he arrived in Montgomery in 1954, Martin spent much of his time finishing up his doctoral dissertation. Hoping to quickly wrap up his degree, Martin had aspirations of becoming a university professor. Deeply intellectual, Martin was as much a philosopher as a pastor. References to Plato were sprinkled throughout his sermons. But he never would make it to the classroom, lecturing before rows of enthralled students. Life had other plans for Martin Luther King Jr.

On December 1, 1955, Rosa Parks refused to give up her seat on a Montgomery city bus. Seizing upon the outrage sparked by Mrs. Parks's arrest, Black civil rights leaders in the community quickly organized and called for a boycott of all city buses. The Black citizens of Montgomery responded, refusing to ride. That initial, enthusiastic response inspired the leaders who called for the boycott to continue indefinitely, until the city leaders of Montgomery responded to their demands to eliminate segregated seating on city buses. But a prolonged boycott would take significant coordination and organizing. Most especially to run and support the extensive carpooling network that would be needed to help the oldest members of the Black community get to and from work each day.

The Montgomery Improvement Association was quickly formed to organize and support the boycott and to represent the Black community in negotiations with the city.

But there was trouble in figuring out who would lead the association. Many of the Black pastors in Montgomery had issues with each other, so there was a reluctance to allow a rival to assume such a high-profile role. So the eyes in the room eventually landed on the newcomer to the group, the intellectual young pastor at Dexter Avenue. Martin accepted the role, but what he didn't know in taking the job was that his plans for a comfortable life of books and lecture halls would come to an end. Thrust into the spotlight, Martin's poise and eloquence would soon capture the attention of the nation, placing him at the center of the burgeoning civil rights movement.

Not everyone was thrilled. Threats were made. Warnings given. Then came the midnight phone call on January 27, 1956. "If you aren't out of this town in three days, we're going to blow up your house and blow your brains out."

The threat pushed Martin to the breaking point. Something in the voice told him that his life was now on the line. And not just his life, but the lives of his wife and their new baby daughter sleeping down the hall.

Wide awake now and unable to go back to bed, Martin made himself some coffee. Fear filled him as he sat down at the table in the dark kitchen. The despair was overwhelming. He began to pray: "Lord, I am here taking a stand for what I believe is right. But now I am afraid. The people are looking to me for leadership, and if I stand before them without strength and courage, they too will falter. I am at the end of my powers. I have nothing left. I've come to the point where I can't face it alone."

In the darkness of that small kitchen, God spoke to Martin. A voice said to him, "Martin Luther, stand up for truth. Stand up for justice. Stand up for righteousness. God will be at your side forever." Hearing those words, the fears evaporated. Resolution, conviction, and courage returned. Sitting alone in the middle of the night, Martin Luther King Jr. responded to God's calling, committing himself to the path of justice and civil rights. It was the decisive moment of his life, the religious experience when Martin Luther King Jr., aspiring college professor, became Martin Luther King Jr., hero and martyr of the American civil rights movement.

We've wrestled with what God's voice is *not* and how to start telling the difference between God's voice and our own. When enchantment baptizes everything we already think and believe, from our nation to our politics to our prejudices, we're worshipping ourselves rather than God. We also need to beware whenever our curated, faddish enchantments only call us to the beautiful, the easy, and the indulgent. If enchantment is just a string of Instagram-worthy moments or always stands on your side of the political aisle, that might not be God's voice you've been paying attention to.

"Discerning the spirits" starts with asking ourselves the hard questions about how our "spirituality" is being used to mask our selfishness and prejudice. But while that hard, honest look in the mirror can tell us when we're *not* hearing the voice of God, we need something else to let us know when we *are* hearing God, how to know when it is Christ who is calling us. We need a test that we can apply to the various enchantments we experience, a test to help us sort God's enchantment from the rest.

Happily, there is such a test, and it's everywhere on display in the Bible. Consider, once again, Moses and the burning bush. We've talked a lot about how Moses had to "turn aside" to see the "strange sight." Let's now focus on what God told Moses as he stood there on holy ground. Moses was given a mission, a sacrificial calling that would consume the rest of his life. Sent to Pharaoh to set the Israelites free, Moses would spend the rest of his days shepherding the children of Israel. The "strange sight" Moses saw wasn't an experience of self-indulgence. It was the exact opposite. The "strange sight" was a call to give his life away for others.

And what a hard calling it was! In leading God's people, there were times when Moses despaired of both sanity and life. I'm sure there were many days when Moses regretted "turning aside" to hear the voice of God.

Over and over again, you see this pattern in Scripture. An encounter with God knocks us out of our comfort zone, if not to lead people like Moses then to cross a bridge to unite a divided people. Remember Peter's vision in Acts 10. Jesus had commissioned his followers to spread the gospel message to the whole world, to all the ethnic groups and nations. But that wasn't happening. The early Jewish Christians were reluctant to cross the ethic boundaries and purity taboos associated with Gentiles. The church had hit a roadblock of ethnic bias and racial prejudice.

So Peter sees a strange sight in Acts 10, a vision of unclean animals lowered from heaven. As we know, the vision wasn't about unclean food but unclean people. The vision was about prejudice and racism. As Peter declares to Cornelius and his household, "God has shown me that I should not call anyone profane or unclean."

Peter's "strange sight" challenged him to face his prejudices. And not just his, but the prejudices of the entire church. Little has changed since Acts 10. We still consider people unclean and unworthy of association. Peter's "strange sight" calls the church, then and now, to the hard work of facing and dismantling what Paul calls the "wall of hostility" that exists between peoples. If we want to "discern the spirits," to sort out if a prompting or calling is coming from God, let's *pay attention to Peter.* When your enchantment causes you to embrace people you have treated as unclean, that looks a whole lot like the work of the Holy Spirit.

The examples of this abound. Think of Jonah. God calls Jonah to preach to the sworn enemies of Israel, the Assyrians. The Assyrians, you'll recall, had raped and pillaged their way through Israel, making slaves of the Israelites and hauling them off into exile. Jonah knows that God is going to forgive the Assyrians if they repent, so he runs the other way. He'd rather not give his enemies a chance at grace. But you know how that story ends. One storm and whale later, Jonah finds himself in Nineveh as an agent of God's grace to a people he hates.

Peter and Jonah illustrate why I hammer so hard on *chosen, curated* enchantments, the enchantments we pick and choose to adorn our lives. When I'm curating dinner party guests or choosing whom to spend my time with, I'm not typically picking hard and difficult people. Peter wouldn't have invited the Gentiles, and Jonah wouldn't have invited the Assyrians. But as we see illustrated over and over again in the Bible, God's enchantment—from visions of unclean animals to being swallowed by whales—drags us toward people we'd rather avoid, even toward the people we hate.

St. Francis of Assisi is one of my favorite examples of God's enchantment. As you may know, Francis had a very enchanted experience with the natural world, a wonderful example of having a sacramental ontology. A beautiful expression of this is found in Francis's Canticle of the Sun, a famous song where he addresses the sun and moon, fire and water, and everything in the natural world, as his sisters and brothers. The Canticle of the Sun has a very Celtic feel to it; St. Patrick would have loved it. Francis was also very fond of animals. If you ever see a statue of St. Francis in a garden, he's always got animals standing around him and birds on his shoulders. Because of all this, St. Francis can strike us as being a bit of a hippie, a flower child right out of the 1960s.

I get that, but this is the story you need to know about St. Francis, which illustrates God's enchantment. After Francis received his calling from God, he'd renounced his family's wealth to live in poverty. At the start, he mainly spent his time repairing old churches. But Francis had a problem he felt was interfering with the mission God had given him. Francis feared and dreaded lepers, who were quite common in the Middle Ages. Their deformity nauseated Francis. The very sight of a leper would send Francis into a panic, causing him to run away. Francis knew his fear and loathing of lepers was antithetical to love and his calling. So one day, upon seeing a leper on the road, Francis rushed up and kissed him. And with that embrace, Francis's fear and dread left him, never to return. Moving down the road, Francis looked back and discovered that the leper had vanished into thin air. Shocked, Francis realized that it was Christ whom he had kissed, his Master appearing to him in the guise of what he dreaded and feared. Rejoicing in the "strange sight,"

Francis began living among and caring for lepers in and around Assisi. Francis's followers, the Franciscan monks, would follow his example, becoming noteworthy in the Middle Ages for their care of lepers.

Just like Peter's vision, God's enchantment drew Francis toward people he feared and loathed. St. Francis may be that lovely statue in a beautiful, curated garden, but the enchantment Francis experienced on the road that day caused him to spend a lot of time in some disgusting, ugly, revolting, and nauseating places. Not a lot of beautiful, Instagram-worthy pics to be found in a leper colony. The enchantment Francis experienced was no Pottery Barn enchantment, all cozy surfaces, warm colors, and twinkling $20 candles. God's enchantment will take you to places where you have to deal with your gag reflex.

When you're looking for God's enchantment, pay attention to St. Francis. The nature-loving Francis *and* the Francis who kissed the leper. God's enchantment will draw you to both the beautiful and the ugly, to delight and disgust, to the easy and the hard. Follow enchantment toward your lepers. That voice you're hearing is the voice of God.

The ultimate test of enchantment, how we "discern the spirits," is clear: sacrificial love, giving yourself for others.

The fancy way to say this is that God's enchantment is *cruciform*, drawing us toward each other in self-giving love. Even for those we fear, loathe, or hate. That's what happened on the cross, after all. While we were God's *enemies*, Christ gave his life *for us*. That's the shape of God's love, what God's enchantment is calling us toward. As Jesus says in the Gospel of Luke, God is kind to the ungrateful and to the wicked. We adore the Celtic vision of God coming to us in the sun and rain, but Jesus points out *the cruciform shape of sun and rain*, the scandal and the shock of God's love. Our Father in heaven, says Jesus, causes the sun and rain to fall upon both the good and the wicked. God's love is unconditional and indiscriminate. So love like the sun and rain, says Jesus, this is the scandalous love that makes you children of your Father in heaven.

Of course, this is very hard. We won't reach this love in our lifetimes. But it's the direction everything in our lives should be pointed toward. God's love is our North Star. The cross is always our compass. Sacrificial love, even for our enemies, is the shape of enchantment when it is Christ who is speaking to us.

That is the test, how we sort God's enchantment from all the noise in this "spiritual but not religious" world. God's enchantment points you toward the cross, toward sacrificial love. Martin Luther King Jr., after he took up the cause of civil rights, always referred to his calling as his "Golgotha," the place where Jesus was crucified. Sitting in fear all alone in the darkness, Martin Luther King Jr. had an "eccentric experience," God calming his fears and giving him courage. But the experience wasn't mere uplift. The enchantment was also cruciform, Martin picking up the cross and setting out for Golgotha, a call to give his life away in service for others.

The voice on the phone that night kept his promise to Martin. Three days after the phone call, the King house was bombed. And twelve years after Martin had his religious experience in the kitchen, he was cut down by an assassin's bullet. He had arrived at his Golgotha. He had fought the good fight and finished his race.

The enchantment that called Martin carried him to the very end. The evening before his death, Martin preached his final sermon. He was reflective and melancholy before the crowd in Memphis that night, as if he sensed his death was near. But he built to a crescendo as he approached the end, the final words he would ever preach:

> Like anybody, I would like to live a long life. Longevity has its place. But I'm not concerned about that now. I just want to do God's will. And He's allowed me to go up to the mountain. And I've looked over. And I've seen the Promised Land.

I may not get there with you. But I want you to know tonight, that we, as a people, will get to the Promised Land!

And so, I'm happy tonight.

I'm not worried about anything.

I'm not fearing any man!

Mine eyes have seen the glory of the coming of the Lord!

For twelve years, Martin had followed the voice of God, carrying his cross. He sensed that his Golgotha was now at hand. And here, at the end, God's enchantment still carried him. In the face of death, he was joyful and courageous. He had looked over and seen the Promised Land, God's hoped-for eucatastrophe. His eyes had seen the glory of the coming of the Lord.

EPILOGUE
HUNTING MAGIC EELS

Eels really are magical, if you learn to look at them correctly. And let me confess, I'm not a big fan of eels. So I have to struggle to see them in the right way. Which is true of most everything in my life. Because of my distaste, boredom, hurry, or stress, I have to practice and work hard to see the world with enchanted eyes.

You'll recall there was a time when I was facing a crossroads and crisis in my faith journey. This skeptical age was hitting me hard. Though I still was attending church, I was mostly checked out. I doubted and had questions about every song and sermon. I'd stopped praying.

During this season, I spent a lot of time investing in my doubts. I say "investing" purposefully. If enchantment is a matter of attention, a willingness to see, I was turning away and closing my eyes. Instead, I cultivated my skepticism. I gathered arguments against God and faith like a butterfly collector. Skeptical books were filling my shelves. Then suddenly, that's all I could see. Piles of questions and a disenchanted, godless world. By paying attention to the ball being passed back and forth, by investing and devoting my attention to my doubts, I no longer could see the dancing gorilla right in front of me. Strange sights were all around, but I stopped turning aside to see them.

During this season of doubt, I heard about some ideas in Fyodor Dostoevsky's novel *The Brothers Karamazov*. The protagonist of the book is Alyosha Karamazov, one of three brothers featured in the story. But the brother I was interested in was Ivan. When the story opens, Alyosha is a novice monk on the verge of taking holy orders. Ivan, though, is an atheist, an evangelist of our skeptical age. In the first part of the book, there's a conversation between Ivan and Alyosha where Ivan tells his believing brother all the reasons a person should become an atheist.

I'd heard that the arguments Ivan makes in the book are some of the best arguments that have ever been made for not believing in God. Keen as I was to invest in my doubts, I picked up the novel to hear what Ivan had to say. Sure enough, Ivan makes powerful, convincing arguments for atheism. Modern-day atheists repeat or rehash Ivan's arguments all the time. I found Ivan absolutely convincing. So I stopped reading and put the novel down. I'd found what I wanted to find, seen what I wanted to see: more ammunition for my growing doubts.

But the novel doesn't end with Ivan's arguments for atheism. If I'd kept reading, I would have found that there is another voice in Alyosha's life that contradicts Ivan's, a voice calling us to see God in this skeptical world. As I mentioned, Alyosha is planning on becoming a monk. In the monastery, Alyosha is a student of the elder Zosima, a very humble and holy man. After his conversation with Ivan, Alyosha goes to hear the final teachings of the elder before he dies. In his final exhortation to his followers and fellow monks, Zosima makes an argument for God and faith.

I'd heard none of this because I'd put the book down before I got to Zosima's final sermon. Again, it's all about attention. Since I was curating my skepticism, I only cared about what Ivan had to say, the arguments against God. All I wanted were my doubts.

I can't recall when all this occurred to me. It was a slow and subtle process. But over time, it dawned on me that my doubts were quite self-imposed, that my questions were products of my *selective attention*, what I had been choosing to look at, read, listen to, or consider. This seems blindingly obvious in retrospect. You are what you eat. And my diet had been given over wholly to the skeptical age.

So I started making different choices with my attention, where I pointed my heart and mind. I've shared with you many of the things I did, from prayer ropes to leaving the Christmas tree up to filling my office with icons to raising my hands in worship at Freedom. As a part of this journey, I picked up *The Brothers Karamazov* once more. I was ready to keep reading. It was time to pay attention to what the elder Zosima had to say, to turn aside and see the strange sight.

Again, after his conversation with Ivan, Alyosha goes to hear the final teachings of Zosima before he dies. Zosima's final sermon is a call to love the world, every last part of it. And when I read this exhortation, I found myself stunned and speechless. I'd finally pushed past my doubts to find words I'd been waiting for my entire life:

> Love all of God's creation, both the whole of it and every grain of sand. Love every leaf, every ray of God's light. Love animals, love plants, love each thing. If you love each thing, you will perceive the mystery of God in things. Once you have perceived it, you will begin tirelessly to perceive more and more of it every day. And you will come at last to love the whole world with an entire, universal love. . . .
>
> Love is a teacher, but one must know how to acquire it, for it is difficult to acquire, it is dearly bought, by long work over a long time, for one ought to love not for a chance moment but for all time. Anyone, even a wicked man, can love by chance. My young brother [once] asked forgiveness of the birds: it seems senseless, yet it is right, for all is like an ocean, all flows and connects; touch it in one place and it echoes at the other end of the world. Let it be madness to ask

forgiveness of the birds, still it would be easier for the birds, and for a child, and for any animal near you, if you yourself were more gracious than you are now, if only by a drop, still it would be easier. All is like an ocean, I say to you.

Love is the enchantment of the world. When we love the world, every grain of it, it shines like transfiguration. Love, as Tolkien said, helps us recover the world, turns everything into a fairy tale. Every leaf, every ray of light. Animals and plants. Mead and good music. The kiss of rain on your skin. The face of a friend and loved one. It all becomes magical. Even the eels.

When we love, we come to "perceive the mystery of God in things." This love is a teacher, a practice of attention and intention. Zosima calls it an act of "perception," the noetic quality described by William James. Love is an apocalypse, a revelation. The willingness to see. The cleaning of the windows. And it's a vision we can choose over and over again, for "once you have perceived it, you will begin tirelessly to perceive more and more of it every day." You keep turning aside to see the strange sight.

This enchantment, Zosima points out, is also cruciform. Even a wicked person can love by chance. God's enchantment, however, calls us to love the hard, the difficult, and the ugly. God's love falls like sun and rain on the entire world. And we are called to contribute our drop, to be more gracious today than we were yesterday. This is a hard-won, cross-shaped love, and it's dearly bought. The price tag is our Golgotha.

And so, dear reader, this is my final encouragement: Love like the sunshine and the rain. Ask forgiveness of the birds. Be a drop more gracious, tender, and kind. Go gently in this mean world. Offer up prayers of Thanks, Help, and Wow. Recover your sacramental wonder. Count your blessings. Look to the horizon in the Valley of Dry Bones. Remember that you are a child of God. Rush to kiss the lepers. Listen to the voice in the night calling you to the cross. Turn your attention to the God dancing right in front of you. God is everywhere present, breathing on this world and turning it to fire. Where you stand is the gateway to heaven. The world is shining like transfiguration. Even the eels.

It only takes a little willingness to see.

ACKNOWLEDGMENTS

Thank you to Emily King at Broadleaf Books for the invitation to write this book, her encouragement, and all her hard editorial work on the manuscript.

Much of the material in this book had its first hearing in my Psychology and Christianity class at Abilene Christian University. In their reactions and responses to the class, my students were the ones who let me know that this material had a resonance and might be worthy of sharing more broadly. Thank you to all my students. I hope reading the book will bring back fond memories of our time together.

Jana and I have dedicated the book to our dear friends Hannah, Gill, and David Bywaters. Our holiday in Wales with Hannah obviously plays a huge part in the book. But the origin of the book goes back to two conversations I had in England during the summer of 2017.

The first conversation occurred after Sunday services at Ashley Church, at lunch at David and Gill's house. During our lovely conversation, surrounded by

David and Gill's garden, Brian Smith made a comment that stopped me in my tracks. We were talking about the declining church attendance in England and the United States, among young people especially. Brian shared that unless we're having an encounter with God at church, there isn't a compelling reason for young people—or anyone—to go. At the time, I had been largely equating Christianity with social justice and believing that such a connection would appeal to my students. But starting with Brian's comment, I increasingly began to wonder if the opposite might be happening, that replacing God with social justice was actually contributing to the decline of faith among my students.

The second conversation was with Hannah during our holiday visiting Glastonbury Abbey with Becky and Reuben. Glastonbury is chock-full of enchantment. From Christianity to King Arthur to ley lines, magical worlds collide in and around the abbey. Noting all this during our visit, Hannah and I began to talk about what we affectionately call the "Faërie people," the wild fusion of hippie, flower child, neopagan, and Celtic spiritualities you find all over the British Isles and especially in Brighton, where Hannah lives. Starting with that holiday in Glastonbury, Hannah and I have had a running conversation about Christianity, the Faërie people, and the vital role of enchantment in our lives.

This book is dedicated to Hannah, Gill, and David. The pages are filled with so many fond memories. Gill's poppies. Holidays with Hannah. And strolling around stately homes with David as we talk about the Bible, history, economics, and politics.